TENNESSEE
COOK BOOK

*Cooking Across America
Cookbook Collection*™

**GOLDEN
WEST** ☼
PUBLISHERS

Front cover photo courtesy National Pork Producers Council.

Back cover photo courtesy of the Country Music Hall of Fame and Museum. Photographer: Timothy Hursley. Architects: Tuck-Hinton Architects.

Acknowledgments

Home and Away: A University Brings Food to the Table— Recipes and Remembrances from East Tennessee State University. (pages 26, 51) Fred Sauceman—East Tennessee State University, Johnson City

Tennessee Department of Agriculture recipes (pages 46, 49) www.picktnproductsorg.

Jesse Colter—"The recipes on pages 25 and 33 are from my private collection and have been provided in fond memory of my husband, Waylon Jennings."

Printed in the United States of America

ISBN – 1-885590-53-9

2nd Printing © 2003

Golden West Publishers, Inc.
4113 N. Longview Ave.
Phoenix, AZ 85014, USA
(800) 658-5830

Visit our website: http://www.goldenwestpublishers.com

Table of Contents

★ ★ ★ ★ *Cooking Across America* ★ ★ ★ ★

Table of Contents (continued)

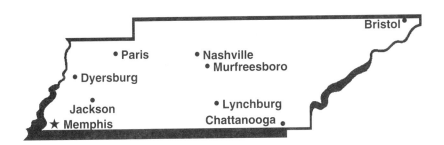

Introduction

Tennessee is not only home to country music, but also to great home-style country cooking. From the Great Smoky Mountains to the Memphis Delta come an abundance of mouth-watering Tennessee dishes—scrumptious breakfasts, hearty main dishes and rich desserts—contributed by homemakers, inns, and Bed and Breakfasts from around the state.

Tennessee Cook Book includes favorite recipes from some of Tennessee's musical legends. Sample Dolly Parton's *Dollywood's Fried Green Tomatoes* or discover how the King of Rock 'n' Roll preferred his hamburger *(Elvis' Hamburger Steak)*.

Jack Daniel's famous Tennessee Whiskey has been produced at Lynchburg since the 1860s. *Tennessee Cook Book* contains several recipes using this Tennessee favorite. Try *Tipsy Sweet Potatoes, Jack's Sweet-Hot Party Pecans,* or *Jack Daniel's Lynchburg Lemonade.*

Tennessee Cook Book also features Southern classics like *Black-Eyed Peas and Ham Hocks, Apple Stack Cake, Baked Country Ham, Sautéed Frog Legs, Crawfish Pie* and many more. You'll also learn creative ways to use cornbread: *Cornbread & Chicken Casserole, Cornbread Salad, Buffalo Chicken Cornbread with Bleu Cheese Mayo,* to name a few.

From appetizers to desserts, we're sure you'll treasure this sampling of Tennessee cuisine!

Tennessee Facts

Size—34th largest state with an area of 42,244 square miles
Population—5,689,283—16th largest state in population
State Capital—Nashville
Statehood—June 1, 1796, the 16th state admitted to the Union
State Name—From a Cherokee Indian village named "Tanasie"
State Nickname—Volunteer State
State Motto—*Agriculture and Commerce*
State Elevations—*Highest:* Clingmans Dome, 6,643 ft.
    Lowest: 178 ft. at the Mississippi River.
State Songs—"My Homeland, Tennessee," "When It's Iris Time in
    Tennessee," "My Tennessee," "Tennessee Waltz," "Rocky Top,"
    "Tennesee" and "The Pride of Tennessee"

 State Bird
Mockingbird

 State Flower
Iris

State Tree
Tulip Poplar

Famous Tennesseans

Eddy Arnold, *singer;* **Chet Atkins,** *guitarist;* **Polly Bergen,** *actress / singer;* **James Bowie,** *knife fighter;* **Jack Garnet Carter,** *miniature golf developer;* **Hattie Caraway,** *first elected woman Senator;* **Davy Crockett,** *frontiersman;* **Sam Davis,** *confederate scout;* **Mark Dean,** *inventor;* **David G. Farragut,** *first American admiral;* **Lester Flatt,** *bluegrass musician;* **Tennessee Ernie Ford,** *singer;* **Morgan Freeman,** *actor;* **Aretha Franklin,** *singer;* **Nikki Giovanni,** *poet;* **Albert Gore Jr.,** *U. S. vice president (1993-2001);* **Red Grooms,** *artist;* **Alex Haley,** *author;* **W. C. Handy,** *known as "Father of the Blues";* **Isaac Hayes,** *composer;* **Barbara Howar,** *broadcaster / writer;* **Sam Houston,** *Governor;* **Andrew Jackson,** *7th U.S. President;* **Andrew Johnson,** *17th U.S. President;* **Estes Kefauver,** *legislator;* **Sondra Locke,** *actress;* **Dolly Parton,** *singer;* **Minnie Pearl,** *singer / comedienne;* **James K. Polk,** *11th U.S. Presi-dent;* **Elvis Presley,** *the "King of Rock 'n' Roll";* **Grantland Rice,** *sportswriter;* **Carl Rowan,** *journalist;* **Sequoia,** *Cherokee scholar / educator;* **Cybil Shepherd,** *actress;* **Dinah Shore,** *actress / singer;* **Bessie Smith,** *Empress of the Blues;* **Tina Turner,** *singer;* **Oprah Winfrey,** *TV talk-show hostess / actress;* **Alvin York,** *WWI hero.*

Tennessee Department of Tourist Development: 1-800-462-8366
Website: http://www.state.tn.us/tourdev

Appetizers
&
Beverages

Ring-of-Fire Layered Dip

"This is a great party snack or appetizer."

Linda Webb—Knoxville

2 cans (9 oz. ea.) BEAN DIP
1 cup PICANTE SAUCE
6 GREEN ONIONS, finely chopped
1 cup MAYONNAISE
1 cup SOUR CREAM

1 cup shredded CHEESE
1 can (4 oz.) sliced BLACK
   OLIVES
JALAPEÑO PEPPERS, diced
TORTILLA CHIPS

Spread bean dip in the bottom of an 8 x 8 pan or large serving dish. Pour picante sauce over bean dip and sprinkle onion over mixture. In a small bowl, blend together mayonnaise and sour cream and then spread mixture over onion. Sprinkle cheese on top; sprinkle olives and peppers over all. Serve with tortilla chips.

Did You Know?

Johnny Cash began his successful recording career in 1956 with Sun Records, backed up by Luther Perkins and Marshall Grant, known as The Tennessee Two.

Artichoke Squares

Norman & Carol Prima—Monteagle Inn, Monteagle

1 can (14 oz.) ARTICHOKE
    HEARTS
1/2 cup OLIVE OIL
2 cloves GARLIC, minced

1/2 cup grated ITALIAN CHEESE
1 cup ITALIAN BREAD CRUMBS
1 EGG

Combine all ingredients and place in a greased 13 x 9 baking pan. Bake at 350° for 30 minutes. Cut into squares and serve.

Imitation Caviar

The Tennessee Aquarium & IMAX 3D Theater—Chattanooga

1 med. EGGPLANT
2 Tbsp. OLIVE OIL
2 cloves GARLIC, minced
2 Tbsp. diced ONION
1/2 tsp. SOY SAUCE

2 Tbsp. minced PARSLEY
1 cup chopped TOMATOES
1 Tbsp. LEMON JUICE
1 tsp. dried BASIL

Cut eggplant in half lengthwise. Bake, cut side down, on a greased cookie sheet at 400° for 60 minutes. As the eggplant cools, gently squeeze out the excess water. Use a spoon to scoop pulp from the skin; place in a bowl and mash with a fork (or place in processor and process until smooth). Add remaining ingredients and blend well. Cover and chill. To serve, spread on **SESAME CRACKERS** and garnish with **chopped HARD-BOILED EGG** and **chopped ONIONS.**

The Tennessee Aquarium

Located in Chattanooga, this is the largest freshwater aquarium in the world! Built with private contributions, this non-profit educational organization is dedicated to the understanding, conservation and enjoyment of the Tennessee River and related ecosystems (visit their website at www.tnaqua.org.)

Jack's Sweet-Hot Party Pecans

A popular party treat!

Jack Daniel's Distillery (www.jackdaniels.com)—Lynchburg

4 Tbsp. BUTTER	**2 Tbsp. TABASCO®**
3 Tbsp. SUGAR	**1 1/2 tsp. SALT**
1/4 cup JACK DANIEL'S®	**1/2 tsp. GARLIC POWDER**
TENNESSEE WHISKEY	**4 cups PECAN HALVES**

Preheat oven to 300°. In a large skillet, combine all ingredients except pecans. Bring to a boil over medium heat, stirring to blend. Boil about 3 minutes. Stir in pecans and toss well to coat. Spread nuts in a single layer in a jelly roll or roasting pan. Bake for 45-60 minutes or until nuts are crisp, stirring occasionally. Cool. Store in an airtight container.

Makes 4 cups.

Did you Know?
Coca-Cola was first bottled in 1899 in Chattanooga.

Mushroom Caviar

Louise B. Howard—Bulls Gap

1 Tbsp. BUTTER or MARGARINE
1/2 med. ONION, minced
1/4 lb. MUSHROOMS, finely chopped
1 Tbsp. LEMON JUICE
SALT and PEPPER
1/2 tsp. WORCESTERSHIRE SAUCE
MAYONNAISE

In a skillet, melt butter, add onion and sauté until golden. Add mushrooms and cook for 5 minutes. Add lemon juice, salt and pepper to taste, and Worcestershire sauce. Stir and then remove from heat. Cool slightly and then stir in enough mayonnaise to hold all together. Mound on a serving plate and chill. Serve with crackers or melba toast.

Southern Bacon Roll-Ups

"A wonderful appetizer for get-togethers!"

Alison Ely—Lakeland

1/4 cup BUTTER	1 EGG, slightly beaten
1/2 cup WATER	1/2 lb. SAUSAGE
1 1/2 cups HERB-SEASONED STUFFING	2/3 lb. sliced BACON

In a saucepan, combine butter with water and heat until butter is melted; remove from heat. Stir in stuffing; add egg and sausage and blend thoroughly. Chill for one hour. Shape mixture into small balls. Cut bacon strips crosswise into thirds. Wrap one piece of bacon around dressing mixture and fasten with toothpick. Place in shallow pan. Bake at 375° for 35 minutes or until brown.

Pigeon Forge

A vacationer's paradise for indoor and outdoor adventure!

Music and comedy entertainments include:
- Elwood Smooch's Ole Smoky Hoedown
- Dixie Stampede
- Black Bear Jamboree
- Comedy Barn Theater
- Classic Country Theater

Cheesy Sausage Bites

Tennessee Pork Producers Association—Murfreesboro

8 EGGS	3 cups shredded MOZZARELLA CHEESE
1/2 cup FLOUR	
1 tsp. BAKING POWDER	3/4 lb. SPICY PORK SAUSAGE, cooked and crumbled
3/4 tsp. SALT	
1 1/2 cups COTTAGE CHEESE	

In a large bowl, beat eggs, add flour, baking powder and salt. Blend thoroughly. Fold in remaining ingredients. Spread out in a greased 9 x 9 baking dish. Bake in a 350° oven for 40 minutes. Remove from oven; let stand 10 minutes. Cut into small squares and serve warm.

Bacon, Lettuce & Tomato Bruschetta

Tennessee Pork Producers Association—Murfreesboro

Topping:
- 8-10 slices BACON, crispy cooked and crumbled
- 1 1/3 cups seeded and chopped ROMA TOMATOES
- 1 cup chopped LEAFY GREEN LETTUCE
- 2 Tbsp. chopped fresh BASIL LEAVES
- 1 clove GARLIC, minced
- 1/4 tsp. SALT
- 1/2 tsp. PEPPER

1/3 cup OLIVE OIL
1/2 pkg. (16 oz.) TWIN FRENCH BREAD LOAVES, cut into 1/4-inch slices

In a bowl, toss together all topping ingredients; set aside. Brush olive oil on both sides of bread slices; place on baking sheet. Bake at 400° for 7 minutes per side or until crisp and golden brown; cool. Spoon about 1 tablespoon topping on each toast round.

Makes 24 appetizers.

Apple Dip

"I often serve this dip with our farm-fresh apples."

Cecileia Shultz—Shultz Farm Foods, Athens

1 pkg. (8 oz.) CREAM CHEESE
3/4 cup BROWN SUGAR
1/4 cup POWDERED SUGAR
1 tsp. VANILLA
2 tsp. MILK

Beat cream cheese until creamy. Beat in sugars; add vanilla and milk. Beat until thoroughly mixed. Serve with freshly sliced apples.

Sweet, Hot & Sour Tennessee Whiskey Meatballs

Jack Daniel's Distillery (www.jackdaniels.com)—Lynchburg

Meatballs:

1 lb. PORK SAUSAGE	1/4 cup MILK
1 lb. GROUND BEEF	1/2 cup finely chopped ONION
1/2 cup DRY BREAD CRUMBS	1/2 tsp. SALT
2 EGGS, beaten	1/2 tsp. BLACK PEPPER

Sauce:

1/2 cup APPLE JELLY
1/4 cup SPICY BROWN MUSTARD
1/4 cup JACK DANIEL'S® TENNESSEE WHISKEY
1 tsp. WORCESTERSHIRE SAUCE
HOT PEPPER SAUCE to taste

Preheat oven to 375°. Combine all meatball ingredients in a large mixing bowl. Blend well with hands. Form mixture into 1 1/2-inch balls. Place on an ungreased baking sheet (with sides) or a jelly roll pan. Bake about 30 minutes or until browned and cooked through. In a large skillet, combine all sauce ingredients. Stir until well-blended. Stir in meatballs, coating them thoroughly with sauce and cook about 5 minutes until sauce has thickened slightly. Serve with toothpicks.

Makes about 50 meatballs.

Visit Jack Daniel's Distillery at Lynchburg!

Jack Daniel built a distillery near Lynchburg's Cave Spring in the 1860s. It is the oldest registered distillery (1866) in the nation. Tour the plant to see whiskey-making in action!

Tennessee Cheddar Cheese Squares

"This recipe evolved when a local company started making Tennessee Cheddar."

Virginia Brown—Knoxville

1 stick MARGARINE	1 cup MILK
1 cup chopped ONION	12 oz. SHARP TENNESSEE
2 cups BISQUICK® MIX	CHEDDAR CHEESE, grated
1 EGG	BACON BITS

Preheat oven to 400°. Grease a 12 x 8 baking pan. In a small skillet, melt half of the margarine and sauté onion until translucent. In a medium bowl, combine Bisquick, egg and milk; add onion mixture and half of the cheese. Pour batter into pan. In a small saucepan, melt remaining margarine and sprinkle over batter. Sprinkle remaining cheese and bacon bits over top. Bake for 20 minutes or until lightly brown. Allow to cool, then cut into squares. Serve warm.

America's Largest Earthquake!

The New Madrid Earthquake, which occurred in the winter of 1811 in northwestern Tennessee, was the largest earthquake in American history. According to archaeologists, the Mississippi river flowed backwards for 3 days, creating the 13,000-acre Reelfoot Lake.

Jack Daniel's Lynchburg Lemonade

Jack Daniel's Distillery (www.jackdaniels.com)—Lynchburg

1 part JACK DANIEL'S®	1 part SOUR MIX
TENNESSEE WHISKEY	2 parts 7-UP® or SPRITE®
1 part TRIPLE SEC	

Combine all ingredients in tall glasses and serve.

Low Sugar Tennessee Tea

Sharon Spears—Fall Branch

1 gal. WATER
4 family-size TEA BAGS
8 oz. PINEAPPLE JUICE
1 pkg. KOOL-AID® SUGAR FREE LEMONADE
13 pkgs. SWEET & LOW®
LEMON SLICES

In a large soup pot, bring water to a boil; remove from heat. Steep tea bags in water for 15 minutes. Stir in pineapple juice, lemonade and Sweet and Low; mix well. Serve with lemon slices on the side.

Sassafras Tea

"Mother sometimes served this tea with supper."

Mae Burke—Fall Branch

Wash and dry **SASSAFRAS TREE ROOTS**. Cut roots into chunks. In a saucepan, bring **4 cups of WATER** to a boil; add roots, cover and let simmer for 30 minutes. Add **SUGAR to taste** and serve hot.

Tennessee Tea

"A favorite in mid-Tennessee for luncheons. It is easy to make and very good!"

Cathrine Brown—Lebanon

1 cup WELCH'S® WHITE GRAPE JUICE
1/2 cup INSTANT TEA
1 cup LEMONADE MIX
1 1/2 cups SUGAR
WATER

Pour all ingredients into a 1 gallon jug. Add enough water to fill the jug and mix well. Serve in tall glasses over ice.

Breakfast & Brunch

Crunchy Pecan French Toast

"We make this with our home-grown pecans and serve it with sweetened wild blackberries that are native to Tennessee."

Sharon Petty—Carriage Lane Inn, Murfreesboro

1 EGG	1/2 cup chopped PECANS
1/2 tsp. NUTMEG	1/2 cup crushed CORN FLAKES
1/2 tsp. CINNAMON	4 slices FRENCH BREAD, cut
1/2 cup MILK	3/4-inch thick
1 tsp. VANILLA	BUTTER
1/4 cup SUGAR	

In a bowl, beat egg, nutmeg and cinnamon together. Add milk, vanilla and sugar and stir well; pour mixture into a shallow dish. Place pecans and corn flakes in separate shallow dishes. Dip bread slices into egg mixture then press into pecans and then corn flakes. In a skillet, melt butter and cook bread slices slowly over low heat for about 3 minutes per side or until golden brown.

Peaches & Cream French Toast

"For almost 10 years, we have been perfecting our breakfast menus to celebrate the Southern tradition of breakfast."

Andrea Beaudet—Hillsboro House Bed & Breakfast, Nashville

3 EGGS
3 Tbsp. PEACH PRESERVES
3/4 cup HALF AND HALF
6 slices BREAD
2 Tbsp. MARGARINE
2 fresh PEACHES, peeled and sliced
POWDERED SUGAR

In a small bowl, combine the eggs and peach preserves together, blending with a fork or whisk. Beat in half and half. Place a single layer of bread slices in an 11 x 7 baking dish. Pour egg mixture over the bread; cover and refrigerate overnight or for several hours. When ready to serve, melt margarine in a skillet, add bread slices and cook over medium-high heat until golden brown on both sides. Place French toast on serving plates, add a dollop of **Peach Butter** to top, arrange peach slices on each and sprinkle all with powdered sugar.

Peach Butter

1/3 cup PEACH PRESERVES   1/2 cup BUTTER, softened

In a blender, combine peach preserves and butter. Blend on high speed until fluffy.

Cheesy Grits

1 1/2 cups WATER   2 Tbsp. MILK
1/2 cup GRITS   1 cup grated CHEDDAR
1/2 tsp. SALT   CHEESE
4 EGGS

In a saucepan, combine water, grits and salt. Cover and cook over low heat for 20 minutes. Beat eggs with milk and add cheese; add to grits and stir over low heat until eggs are cooked and cheese has melted.

East Park Inn Brunch Casserole

"Our menus are planned by nationally known cookbook author and TV cooking personality, Daisy King."

Brooks Parker—East Park Inn, An Urban Bed & Breakfast, Nashville

2 lbs. SAUSAGE
1/2 cup chopped GREEN ONIONS
1 can (2 oz.) chopped PIMENTOS
12 slices BREAD, crusts removed
6 EGGS
3 cups MILK
1/4 tsp. DRY MUSTARD
1 Tbsp. WORCESTERSHIRE
    SAUCE
MUSHROOMS, as desired

Place sausage in a skillet and cook until crumbly; drain well. Add onions and pimentos and sauté until tender. Layer half of the bread slices in a buttered 13 x 9 casserole dish. Sprinkle meat and onion mixture over all. Add top layer of bread slices. In a bowl, beat together eggs, milk, mustard and Worcestershire sauce, stir in mushrooms to taste. Pour over top of bread. Refrigerate for 12 hours or overnight. Bake in a 350° oven for 1 1/4 hours.

Serves 12.

Hoe Cakes

"These can be served for breakfast with eggs or as a side dish with almost any meal."

Virginia P. Waters—Lebanon

1 cup CORNMEAL
1/2 cup FLOUR
1 tsp. (heaping) BAKING POWDER
1/4 tsp. BAKING SODA
1 tsp. SALT
1 Tbsp. SUGAR
1 1/2 cups BUTTERMILK
OIL

Combine cornmeal, flour, baking powder, baking soda, salt and sugar. Add enough buttermilk to make batter consistency of pancake batter. Heat griddle or skillet; add oil and using a ladle, add batter for cakes of desired size. Cook until golden brown on both sides.

Strawberry Crepes

"When we decided to open our Bed and Breakfast, my husband and I reviewed our 'family' recipes. One unusual recipe we found was this, the Hotchkiss family crepes. We added strawberry filling and strawberry sauce to the original version."

Judy & Robert Hotchkiss—Prospect Hill Bed & Breakfast Inn,
Mountain City

6 EGGS
4 tsp. SUGAR
1 tsp. SALT
2 cups FLOUR, sifted
2 cups MILK
1 1/2 cups chopped fresh STRAWBERRIES
MINT or PARSLEY SPRIGS for garnish

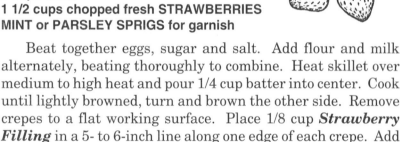

Beat together eggs, sugar and salt. Add flour and milk alternately, beating thoroughly to combine. Heat skillet over medium to high heat and pour 1/4 cup batter into center. Cook until lightly browned, turn and brown the other side. Remove crepes to a flat working surface. Place 1/8 cup **Strawberry Filling** in a 5- to 6-inch line along one edge of each crepe. Add a layer of strawberries, then roll up crepes and place on serving plates. Pour (or paint) a stripe of **Strawberry Sauce** along length of each crepe. Garnish with mint or parsley sprigs.

Serves 6.

Strawberry Filling

3 ctn. (10 oz. ea.) frozen STRAWBERRIES in juice
1/4-1/3 cup SOUR CREAM

Defrost strawberries overnight. Warm thoroughly in microwave and then mash and drain through a sieve. Reserve juice. Stir sour cream to taste into mashed berries.

Strawberry Sauce

Place reserved strawberry juice in a microwaveable container. Add **3 Tbsp. CORNSTARCH** and whisk together. Microwave in short intervals until sauce thickens, stirring often.

Carrot-Nut Pancakes

"A favorite breakfast at our Inn."

Andrea Beaudet—Hillsboro House Bed & Breakfast, Nashville

1 1/2 cups FLOUR	2 EGGS
1 tsp. BAKING POWDER	1 cup BUTTERMILK
1/2 tsp. SALT	2 Tbsp. melted BUTTER or
1/2 tsp. BAKING SODA	VEGETABLE OIL
2 Tbsp. SUGAR	1/2 cup grated CARROTS
1/2 tsp. CINNAMON	1/2 cup chopped NUTS

In a bowl, sift together flour, baking powder, salt, baking soda, sugar and cinnamon. In another bowl, beat eggs, then add buttermilk and beat again. Combine flour and egg mixtures. Add butter and beat well. Fold in carrots and nuts. Set aside for at least one hour. Lightly oil a skillet or griddle and place over medium heat. Pour 2 tablespoons of batter per pancake onto the pan and cook until bubbles appear, begin to break and pancake is golden brown. Turn and brown the other side.

Makes 12-15 pancakes.

Polk Greens & Scrambled Eggs

Sharon Spears—Fall Branch

1 gal. POLK GREENS
1/2 cup BACON DRIPPINGS
1 tsp. SALT
1/4 tsp. PEPPER
6 EGGS

Thoroughly wash polk greens. Place greens in a saucepan with a small amount of water and parboil for 2-3 minutes; using a colander, drain and then rinse and drain again. In a medium skillet, heat bacon drippings; add polk greens, salt and pepper. Cover and cook over medium heat for 25 minutes, stirring occasionally. In a separate bowl, beat eggs; add to polk greens and stir constantly until eggs are cooked.

Egg-Stuffed Baked Tomatoes

"This is an easy-to-make breakfast or brunch favorite!"

Vikki Woods—Iron Mountain Inn B & B and Creekside Chalet, Butler

1 med. TOMATO

Stuffing:
   2 Tbsp. VIRGIN OLIVE OIL
   1/4 cup grated PARMESAN CHEESE
   1/4 cup finely chopped ONION
   1 clove GARLIC, minced
   2 Tbsp. finely chopped PARSLEY
   2 Tbsp. finely chopped CHIVES
   SALT and PEPPER

1 EGG
PARMESAN CHEESE
WATERCRESS for garnish

Preheat oven to 350°. Cut off top of tomato; remove pulp and stand the shell upside down to drain. Finely chop pulp and trimmings from around the top of tomato. In a bowl, combine stuffing ingredients with pulp and mix well. Spread pulp mixture in an individual ramekin; arrange tomato shell on top. Break egg into tomato shell. Sprinkle top with a small amount of parmesan cheese and bake for about 20 minutes or until egg is cooked to desired doneness. Garnish with watercress.

Serves 1.

Cornmeal Mush

Carmela Peterson—Erwin

4 1/2 cups WATER   **2 cups CORNMEAL**   **SALT**

In a medium saucepan, bring water to a boil; stir in cornmeal and salt to taste. Cook over medium heat, stirring until thickened. Serve warm.

Note: Spread leftover mush in a greased pan; chill. When ready to serve, slice and fry until golden brown on both sides.

French Banana Pancakes

"This is a light, yet filling, breakfast treat!"

Lillian J. Katzbeck—Calico Inn, Sevierville

Pancakes:

1 cup ALL-PURPOSE FLOUR	3 Tbsp. BUTTER or
1/4 cup POWDERED SUGAR	MARGARINE, melted
1 cup MILK	1 tsp. VANILLA
2 EGGS, beaten	1/4 tsp. SALT

Sauce:

1/4 cup BUTTER or MARGARINE	1/4 tsp. NUTMEG
1/4 cup packed BROWN SUGAR	1/4 cup LIGHT CREAM
1/4 tsp. CINNAMON	

5-6 firm BANANAS, halved lengthwise
WHIPPED CREAM
Dash of CINNAMON

In a mixing bowl, combine flour and sugar and then stir in remaining pancake ingredients. Beat until smooth. In a 6-inch lightly oiled skillet, over medium heat, add 3 tablespoons batter, spreading to almost cover the bottom of the skillet. Cook pancake until lightly browned; turn and brown the other side. Remove pancake to a wire rack and repeat with remaining batter adding oil as needed. To make sauce: Melt butter in large skillet. Add remaining sauce ingredients and cook until lightly thickened. Add half of the bananas at a time to skillet and heat for 2-3 minutes, spooning sauce over top and turning to cover all sides. Roll each pancake around a banana half and place on serving platter. Spoon remaining sauce over all. Top each pancake roll with a dollop of whipped cream and a dash of cinnamon.

Tennessee Titans

In November 1998, Owner Bud Adams Jr. announced that the Oilers (formerly of Houston) would become the "Tennessee Titans" beginning in 1999. Adams wanted a new nickname to reflect strength, leadership and other heroic qualities.

French Toast Casserole

"This is one of our guests' favorite recipes!"

Norman & Carol Prima—Monteagle Inn, Monteagle

1 pkg. (8 oz.) CREAM CHEESE	1 cup MILK
15 EGGS	1 loaf BREAD, sliced and cut
1 cup SUGAR	into small squares
1 cup HONEY	POWDERED SUGAR
1/8 cup VANILLA	

Place cream cheese in a bowl and whip until fluffy. Add eggs, sugar, honey, vanilla and milk and whip thoroughly. Dip bread squares into cream cheese mixture and place them in a greased, 3-quart casserole dish. Add cream cheese mixture to dish until it is 1/3 full. Refrigerate for 12 hours or overnight. Place dish in a 325° oven and bake for 1-1 1/2 hours. Sprinkle top with powdered sugar and serve with syrup on the side.

Bristol

Brass markers down the center of State Street, Bristol's main thoroughfare, denote the dividing line between Virginia and Tennessee! Bristol's Birthplace of Country Music Alliance Museum memorializes recording artists such as the Carter Family and Jimmie Rodgers and the early radio days of Lester Flatt and Earl Scruggs.

Chocolate Biscuit Gravy

"This is something different for breakfast."

Sharon Spears—Fall Branch

1 cup SUGAR	2 cups MILK
1 Tbsp. (heaping) COCOA	1 tsp. VANILLA
4 tsp. FLOUR	2 Tbsp. BUTTER
WATER	

In a skillet, mix sugar, cocoa and flour together; add enough water to make a paste. Cook over medium heat, adding milk and stirring until mixture has thickened. Remove from heat and stir in vanilla and butter. Serve over biscuits.

Tennessee Brunch

Tennessee Egg & Poultry Association—Murfreesboro

1/4 cup BUTTER or MARGARINE
1/4 cup ALL-PURPOSE FLOUR
2 cups MILK
1/4 tsp. SALT
1/8 tsp. WHITE PEPPER
6-8 HARD-BOILED EGGS, chopped
1/2 cup MAYONNAISE
8 CORNBREAD MUFFINS or SQUARES
8 slices BACON, cooked crisp and crumbled
3/4 cup shredded CHEDDAR CHEESE
Chopped GREEN ONIONS with tops

In a saucepan, melt butter over low heat; add flour, stirring constantly until smooth. Gradually add milk and cook, stirring constantly until thickened and bubbly. Add salt, pepper, eggs and mayonnaise and blend well. Cook over medium heat until thoroughly heated. Slice cornbread muffins in half horizontally. Arrange halves on plates and spoon egg mixture over top. Sprinkle with bacon, cheese and onions.

Understanding Tennesseeans

"I thought you might like to include these. Some of them are purty funny!"

Darlene Wilson—Newport

moe tail—motel
hee yull—hill
rat fur piece—far
far—fire
tail—tell
plum tard—fatigued
prar meeting—church service
mucha bliged—thank you
backer feelt—tobacco field
wekum waggin—welcome wagon
holler—a small community
valley—a small community with a post office
cat heads—big homemade buiscuits
sorghum molasses—something you sop your biscuit into

barnt up—angry
tear out—run
ov air—over there
up air—up there
back air—back there
dawg—dog
naw—disagree
u uns—group of people
tater—potato
mater—tomato

World's Best Baked Oatmeal

"We like to add a wide variety of fresh fruits to this dish!"

Karan Bailey—Huckleberry Inn Bed & Breakfast, Sevierville

1/4 cup OIL
1/4 cup packed BROWN SUGAR
2 EGGS
3 cups OLD-FASHIONED OATS
2 tsp. BAKING POWDER
1/2 tsp. SALT
1 1/4 cups MILK

1 tsp. CINNAMON
LIQUID FRENCH VANILLA
  COFFEE CREAMER
Chopped fresh FRUIT
Chopped PECANS
HONEY

In a bowl, cream oil, brown sugar and eggs together. Add oats, baking powder, salt, milk and cinnamon. Pour into a greased 11 x 8 baking dish. Bake at 350° for 30 minutes. Add oatmeal to serving bowls and sprinkle with additional brown sugar. Add just enough vanilla creamer to cover and pile on fruit. Top with pecans and drizzle with honey.

Serves 4.

Three U. S. Presidents Lived in Tennessee

James Polk (1845-1849) lived in Mecklenburg County, Andrew Jackson (1829-1837) in Union County and Andrew Johnson (1865-1869) in Greene County.

Tennessee Mountaintop Bacon

"At the Von-Bryan, we like to sit on the porch and look across the valley to the Great Smoky Mountains!"

Jo Ann Vaughn—Von Bryan Mountaintop Inn, Sevierville

1/2 cup FLOUR
1/4 cup packed BROWN SUGAR

1 tsp. BLACK PEPPER
1 lb. COUNTRY-STYLE BACON

In a bowl, combine flour, sugar and pepper together. Dredge bacon in flour mixture to cover both sides. Pan fry or bake in a 325° oven until brown and crisp.

Soups & Salads

Waylon's Corn Chowder

"This recipe from my private collection was one of Waylon's summer favorites. When the corn was truly fresh, he loved it served for lunch with a barbecue sandwich or cornbread."

Mrs. Waylon Jennings (Jessi Colter)—Brentwood

1/2 lb. BACON
1 lg. ONION, diced
1 cup diced CELERY
1/2 cup ALL-PURPOSE FLOUR
2 qts. CHICKEN STOCK
2 cups diced POTATOES
1/2 tsp. THYME
1 BAY LEAF
4 sprigs PARSLEY

6 PEPPERCORNS, crushed
1 clove GARLIC
6 ears SWEET CORN
   or 2 cups CORN
2 Tbsp. BUTTER
2 cups HALF AND HALF
SALT and PEPPER
PARSLEY SPRIGS for
   garnish

In a 4-quart stock pot, sauté bacon until fat is rendered. With a slotted spoon, remove bacon and discard it, leaving the fat in the pot. Add onion and celery and sauté until onion is translucent. Add flour and continue to cook over low heat for 10 minutes. Add chicken stock and bring mixture to a boil, stirring until no lumps remain. Reduce heat to a simmer; add potatoes, thyme, bay leaf, parsley, peppercorns and garlic. Cut corn from cobs and add to the pot. Continue simmering until potatoes are tender. Add butter and half and half; return to a simmer. Season with salt and pepper to taste. Ladle chowder into bowls and garnish with parsley.

Bacon-Clam Chowder

"I love chowder and was looking for a recipe that was quick and easy. This is one of my own creations."

Nellie deBruycker—Crossville

6 slices BACON	1 can (10 oz.) BABY CLAMS
2 med. ONIONS, chopped	SALT and PEPPER
2 med. POTATOES, diced	Chopped PARSLEY
1 cup WATER	1 sm. TOMATO, chopped
2 cups MILK	

In a large saucepan, cook bacon; drain, crumble and set aside. In the same saucepan, sauté onions in bacon drippings until translucent; add potatoes and water. Cover and simmer over low heat for 8 minutes; stir in milk, clams, salt and pepper to taste and heat thoroughly. Garnish with parsley and tomato.

Black-Eyed Peas & Ham Hocks

"Black-eyed peas, or cowpeas, were first brought to this country from Africa in 1674. This recipe is from 'Home and Away: A University Brings Food to the Table—Recipes and Remembrances from East Tennessee State University.'"

Fred Sauceman—East Tennessee State University, Johnson City

1/2 lb. BLACK-EYED PEAS	2 stalks CELERY,
2 or 3 SMOKED HAM HOCKS	coarsely chopped
1 lg. ONION, coarsely chopped	SALT and PEPPER
1 GREEN BELL PEPPER,	1/2 tsp. crushed RED
coarsely chopped	PEPPER FLAKES

Soak black-eyed peas for 4 hours. Place ham hocks in large pot, add enough water to just cover and bring to a boil. Reduce heat, cover and simmer for 1 1/2 hours until meat is tender. Add drained black-eyed peas and remaining ingredients and continue to cook for 1-1 1/2 hours longer or until vegetables are tender. Remove ham hocks and pull meat off the bone; return meat to the stew. Cook, uncovered, until liquid is reduced and stew is slightly thickened.

Taco Stew

Annie Sue Whited—Lebanon

1 lb. GROUND BEEF
1 med. ONION, chopped
1 can (10.75 oz.) TOMATO SOUP
1 can (15 oz.) WHOLE KERNEL CORN
1 can (15 oz.) CHILI BEANS
1 can (16 oz.) TOMATOES WITH CHILES
1 pkg. (1.25 oz.) TACO SEASONING MIX
1 cup WATER

In a skillet, brown beef and onion; drain fat from skillet and add remaining ingredients. Bring mixture to a boil and then simmer for 10 minutes. Serve with **TORTILLA CHIPS** and **shredded MONTEREY JACK CHEESE.**

Shelbyville

Besides being home to manufacturers of writing instruments such as Musgrave and Sanford, this city celebrates the Tennessee Walking Horse National Celebration. Many of these famed horses are raised and trained in the surrounding area.

Soup for the Slopes

Imogene M. Engle—Knoxville

1 lb. SAUSAGE
1 lg. ONION, diced
1 sm. GREEN BELL PEPPER, diced
1 BAY LEAF
1 can (28 oz.) TOMATOES
4-6 POTATOES, peeled and cubed
2 cans (15 oz. ea.) PINTO or KIDNEY BEANS
SALT and PEPPER

In a skillet, brown sausage and onion; drain well. Add remaining ingredients, seasoning with salt and pepper to taste and simmer 40 minutes. Add water for desired consistency. Remove bay leaf before serving.

Catfish Chowder

Large firm CATFISH BONES
5 cups WATER
2 tsp. SALT
4 med. POTATOES, diced
1 can (16 oz.) diced TOMATOES
2 ONIONS, diced
1/4 tsp. PEPPER
2 lbs. CATFISH FILLETS, diced
1 Tbsp. LEMON JUICE
1 Tbsp. chopped PARSLEY

Add catfish bones, water and salt to a saucepan. Bring to a boil, reduce heat and let simmer for 10 minutes. Remove and discard bones. Add potatoes, tomatoes, onions and pepper to saucepan. Bring to a boil, then simmer until potatoes are tender. Add fish and cook until it flakes. Stir in lemon juice and parsley just before serving.

Salmon Toss

"This is a much requested luncheon dish."

Elaine Tubb Wingerter—Ernest Tubb Record Shop #1, Nashville

1/2 cup MAYONNAISE
1/8 tsp. CHILI POWDER
1/8 tsp. CURRY POWDER
1/8 tsp. CORIANDER
3 Tbsp. LEMON JUICE
1 can (15.25 oz.) RED SALMON, drained, skinned, boned & flaked
1/2 cup chopped GREEN BELL PEPPER
1/4 cup sliced GREEN ONIONS
1/2 cup slivered ALMONDS or PECANS
2 APPLES
LETTUCE or SPINACH LEAVES

In a bowl, combine mayonnaise and spices and stir well; add 1 tablespoon of lemon juice. In another bowl, combine salmon, bell pepper, green onions and almonds. Peel and cube one apple, place in a separate bowl and sprinkle with remaining lemon juice. Pour mayonnaise mixture over salmon mixture and then the apples; mix salmon and apples thoroughly. Refrigerate at least 2 hours. Serve on a bed of lettuce or spinach leaves. Garnish with slices of the remaining apple.

Grammy's Cranberry Salad

"A holiday tradition in our family, this dish is as important as the turkey or ham."

Alison Ely—Lakeland

1 lb. CRANBERRIES
1 1/2 cups SUGAR
2 cups MINIATURE
    MARSHMALLOWS
1 cup chopped PECANS

1 can (20 oz.) CRUSHED
    PINEAPPLE, drained
1 pint WHIPPING CREAM,
    whipped

Grind cranberries and place in a bowl; stir in sugar and let stand overnight. Place marshmallows in another bowl and pour cranberry mixture over marshmallows. Fold in pecans, pineapple and whipped cream.

Maryville's Renowned Sam Houston

Sam Houston resigned as Governor of Tennessee in 1829. He later became President of the Republic of Texas and served as Governor of Texas when statehood was granted. He was the 7th Governor of both Tennessee and Texas. The log schoolhouse where he taught school at Maryville (1811-1812) still stands and is a State Historic Site.

Okra Salad

1 lb. sm. OKRA PODS
1/2 cup thinly sliced SWEET
    ONIONS

1 clove GARLIC, minced
4 TOMATOES, sliced

Blanch okra in boiling water for 3 minutes. Drain. Combine okra, onion and garlic in a bowl. Pour **Dressing** over top; toss to coat and marinate in refrigerator for at least 2 hours. When ready to serve, line serving plates with tomato slices and mound drained okra mixture in center.

Dressing

1/4 cup OLIVE OIL
1/4 cup VEGETABLE OIL
1/4 cup BALSAMIC VINEGAR

1/2 tsp. TABASCO
SALT and PEPPER to taste

In a bowl, combine all dressing ingredients; whisk.

Crunchy Pea Salad

"This recipe is attractive and delicious. I have used it for years and like it because I can make it a day or two ahead of time."

Nellie deBruycker—Crossville

1 cup RANCH DRESSING
1/2 cup SOUR CREAM
1/2 tsp. DRY DILL
1/4 tsp. PEPPER
1 pkg. (16 oz.) frozen PEAS, thawed and drained
1 cup chopped, fresh CAULIFLOWER
1 cup chopped CELERY
1 cup slivered ALMONDS
1/4 cup finely diced GREEN ONIONS
1/4 cup finely diced RADISHES, optional

In a large bowl, combine ranch dressing, sour cream, dill and pepper; add remaining ingredients and stir gently to coat. Chill well before serving.

Note: If made in advance, do not add onion until the day salad is to be served.

Apple & Nut Salad

"Though mostly served at Thanksgiving and Christmas, my mother occasionally gave in at the urging of my brother and me and made this at other times."

Elaine Tubb Wingerter—Ernest Tubb Record Shop #1, Nashville

2 EGGS, beaten
4 Tbsp. SUGAR
4 Tbsp. LEMON JUICE
6 cups peeled and diced APPLES*
1/2-1 cup chopped PECANS

In a saucepan, combine eggs, sugar and lemon juice. Cook over medium heat until mixture thickens to the consistency of eggnog. Pour mixture over apples and pecans; mix well. If apples are not well-coated, repeat the sauce recipe. Cover and refrigerate for at least 2 hours.

*Note: Sprinkle lemon juice over apples to keep from browning.

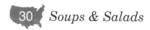

Cornbread Salad

Tina Stacy—Fall Branch

3 cups crumbled CORNBREAD
1 sm. GREEN BELL PEPPER, chopped
2 HARD-BOILED EGGS, chopped
4 slices BACON, cooked and crumbled
1 med. TOMATO, diced
1 sm. SWEET ONION, chopped
1/2 cup MAYONNAISE
1 Tbsp. VINEGAR

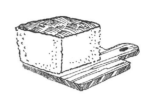

In a mixing bowl, combine cornbread, bell pepper, eggs, bacon, tomato and onion and mix lightly. In another bowl, combine mayonnaise and vinegar and blend. Pour over cornbread mixture and mix thoroughly.

Tennessee Fact Sampler

- *Kingston served as the state capital for one day (Sept. 21, 1807). A two-hour legislative session passed two resolutions and then adjourned back to Knoxville.*
- *President Andrew Johnson held every elective office at the local, state and federal level.*
- *Thoroughbred Secretariat traces his bloodline to Iroquois, who was bred at Nashville's Belle Meade Plantation.*

Strawberry-Spinach Salad

Karan Bailey—Huckleberry Inn Bed & Breakfast, Sevierville

Dressing:
1/3 cup MAYONNAISE
1/4 cup UNSWEETENED ORANGE JUICE
1 tsp. SUGAR
1 tsp. POPPY SEEDS

1/2 lb. fresh SPINACH, washed, trimmed and torn
2 cups sliced fresh STRAWBERRIES

Combine dressing ingredients in a small bowl; stir well and set aside. In a large bowl, gently toss spinach and strawberries together. Arrange portions of spinach mixture on 8 salad plates and drizzle 1 tablespoon dressing over each.

Rocky Top Tomato Salad

"This was a Tennessee State Fair Blue Ribbon Winner!"

Cathrine Brown—Lebanon

2 cups chopped TOMATOES
1/2 cup chopped CELERY
2/3 cup chopped SWEET ONION
1 Tbsp. LEMON JUICE
1/4 tsp. SALT

1 pkg. (1 oz.) PLAIN GELATIN
1/4 cup COLD WATER
1 pkg. (3 oz.) LEMON JELL-O®
PARSLEY

In a saucepan, combine first 5 ingredients and bring to a boil; reduce heat and simmer for 5 minutes, stirring occasionally. In a bowl, combine plain gelatin and water and let soften. Stir lemon Jell-O and gelatin into saucepan mixture and mix thoroughly. Remove from heat and refrigerate until partially set. Coat inside of a deep bowl with cooking oil. Pour tomato mixture into bowl and chill until completely set; unmold onto serving plate and spread sides and top with ***Rocky Top Snow.*** Garnish with parsley. Refrigerate at least 1 hour or overnight.

Rocky Top Snow

1 pkg. (8 oz.) CREAM CHEESE
3/4 cup MAYONNAISE
1 tsp. CELERY SEED

1 Tbsp. LEMON JUICE
2/3 cup chopped SWEET
ONION

In a bowl, combine all ingredients together thoroughly.

Sauerkraut Salad

"You will find this in my refrigerator most of the time. This is delicious with soup, beans, meat or potatoes."

Mae Burke—Fall Branch

2 cans (14 oz. ea.) SAUERKRAUT
1 cup diced CELERY
1 med. GREEN BELL
PEPPER, diced
1 sm. ONION, diced
1 can (4 oz.) PIMENTOS

1/2 cup SALAD OIL
1/2 cup VINEGAR
1 cup SUGAR
1 Tbsp. WORCESTERSHIRE
SAUCE

Chop sauerkraut, place in a bowl and add all remaining ingredients. Mix well. Cover and refrigerate overnight.

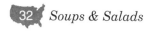

Main Dishes

Mama's Goulash

"This is a recipe that Waylon's mother prepared for the family when he was a child. It's from my private collection."

Mrs. Waylon Jennings (Jessi Colter)—Brentwood

1 Tbsp. COOKING OIL
1 1/2 lbs. GROUND ROUND
1/2 cup chopped ONION
1/4 cup chopped GREEN BELL PEPPER
1/2 tsp. GARLIC SALT
1 tsp. CHILI POWDER
1 Tbsp. PICANTE SAUCE
2 cans (8 oz. ea.) TOMATO SAUCE
1 Tbsp. SUGAR
1 box (8 oz.) ELBOW MACARONI

In a large skillet, heat oil; add meat and cook until no longer pink. Add onion, bell pepper, garlic salt, chili powder and picante sauce. Cook until onion is translucent. Stir in tomato sauce and sugar; simmer for 20 minutes. Cook macaroni according to directions on package; drain well. Add macaroni to meat mixture and stir well. Simmer for an additional 5-10 minutes.

Baked Vegetable Casserole

"This Mediterranean-style casserole needs only some crusty bread to accompany it!"

Karan Bailey—Huckleberry Inn Bed & Breakfast, Sevierville

1 lg. bunch BROCCOLI, cut into small pieces
3 med. POTATOES, peeled and cut into 1-inch chunks
1 can (28 oz.) TOMATOES, finely chopped and well-drained
1 can (15 oz.) CANNELLINI (white) BEANS, rinsed and drained
1/2 cup pitted BLACK OLIVES, halved
2 1/2 Tbsp. OLIVE OIL
2 cloves GARLIC, minced
1/4 tsp. crushed RED PEPPER FLAKES
SALT
1 1/4 cups grated MUENSTER CHEESE

Bring a 3-quart saucepan of water to a boil. Blanch broccoli for 2 minutes, or until tender yet still crunchy. Remove from pan and plunge into a bowl of cold water to stop cooking. Drain well and pat dry. Place broccoli in a large bowl. In a saucepan, add potatoes and water to cover; cook until tender (about 7 minutes). Drain potatoes well and add to the broccoli. Stir in tomatoes, beans and olives. In a bowl, combine olive oil, garlic and red pepper flakes, pour over vegetables and toss gently to coat. Season with salt to taste. Preheat oven to 400°. Spread half of the vegetable mixture in a 12 x 7 x 2 casserole dish. Sprinkle top with half of the cheese. Add remaining vegetables and top with remaining cheese. Cover dish with foil, place in oven and bake for 30 minutes. Remove foil and bake for an additional 5 minutes or until crust is golden.

Early Tennessee Explorers

The first white man to come to Tennessee was the Spanish explorer Hernando de Soto in 1540. In the late 1600s, James Needham and Gabriel Arthur of England and Louis Joliet of Canada and Father Jacques Marquette of France also explored the region.

Hernando de Soto

Buffalo Chicken Cornbread with Bleu Cheese Mayo

This recipe, submitted by Diane Sparrow, was a 1st place winner in the National Cornbread Festival 2002 Cornbread Cook-Off sponsored by Lodge Manufacturing and Martha White®.

National Cornbread Festival—South Pittsburg

1 lb. CHICKEN BREAST TENDER STRIPS
1/4 cup LOUISIANA-STYLE HOT SAUCE
3 Tbsp. BUTTER
1/2 cup chopped RED ONION
1/2 cup chopped CELERY
1 pkg. MARTHA WHITE® COTTON PICKIN' CORNBREAD MIX
1/2 cup MILK
1 EGG

Preheat oven to 450°. Place chicken strips in a bowl, toss with hot sauce to coat and set aside to marinate for 20 minutes. Melt 1 tablespoon of butter in a 10-inch cast iron skillet over medium heat. Sauté the onion and celery until tender; remove from skillet. Add remaining butter to skillet; add chicken and sauté for 5-7 minutes, stirring constantly. In a bowl, combine cornbread mix with milk and egg; stir in onion and celery. Pour cornbread mixture over chicken in hot skillet. Place skillet in preheated oven and bake for 20-25 minutes or until cornbread is golden brown. Cut cornbread into wedges, place on serving plates and top each with *Bleu Cheese Mayo.*

Serves 6.

Bleu Cheese Mayo

1/2 cup MAYONNAISE   **1/2 tsp. SALT**
1/4 cup PLAIN YOGURT   **2 tsp. LEMON JUICE**
2 oz. BLEU CHEESE, crumbled

In a bowl, combine all ingredients, cover and refrigerate until ready to serve.

Additional information about the festival can be found at:
www.nationalcornbread.com or www.lodgemfg.com.

Cajun-Style Catfish

The Tennessee Aquarium & IMAX 3D Theater—Chattanooga

Seasonings:
1 Tbsp. PAPRIKA
2 1/2 tsp. SALT
3/4 tsp. PEPPER
1 tsp. ONION POWDER
1/2 tsp. dried THYME LEAVES
1 tsp. GARLIC POWDER
1/2 tsp. MARJORAM

6 CATFISH FILLETS
1/2 lb. UNSALTED BUTTER, melted
6 Tbsp. BUTTER
LEMON WEDGES

Fire up the grill. In a small bowl, combine seasoning ingredients. Dip fillets in melted butter, then sprinkle seasoning mix on both sides. Place each fillet on an 18 x 18 inch section of heavy-duty aluminum foil. Add a tablespoon of butter to top of each fillet and wrap in foil. When grill coals are white hot, place wrapped fish on the grill about 6 inches above the heat. Cook for 10-15 minutes, or until the fish flakes easily. Serve with lemon wedges.

Hot Hominy

Alease Irvine—Memphis

1 lb. BULK PORK SAUSAGE
2 med. ONIONS, chopped
1 GREEN BELL PEPPER, chopped
2 cans (14.5 oz. ea.) WHITE HOMINY, drained
1 can (14.5 oz.) TOMATOES WITH GREEN CHILES
1 Tbsp. WORCESTERSHIRE SAUCE
Dash of TABASCO®
Dash of RED PEPPER
SALT & PEPPER
2 cups grated CHEDDAR CHEESE

In a skillet, cook sausage, onions and bell pepper until sausage is no longer pink. Drain fat. Add hominy, tomatoes and seasonings; heat thoroughly. In a greased casserole dish, alternate layers of hominy mixture and cheese, ending with cheese on top. Bake at 350° for 15-20 minutes or until cheese is bubbly.

Shepherd's Pie

"This recipe comes from the 'Recipes From Rugby' cookbook,
published by Historic Rugby Press."

Barbara Stagg—Historic Rugby Visitor Center, Rugby

1/4 cup MARGARINE	1/2 tsp. SAGE
1 cup chopped ONIONS	1 tsp. GARLIC POWDER
4 cups thinly sliced CARROTS	1 tsp. SALT
1 cup chopped CELERY	PEPPER
10 cups (1/2-inch pieces) cooked	3 lg. BAY LEAVES
ROAST BEEF or POT ROAST	3 lg. POTATOES, peeled,
2 cups BROWN GRAVY	boiled and mashed
1 BEEF BOUILLON CUBE	1 cup grated CHEDDAR
3 tsp. PARSLEY FLAKES	CHEESE

In a large skillet, melt margarine; add onions, carrots and celery and sauté until just tender. Add roast beef, gravy and spices and simmer slowly for about 20 minutes. Remove bay leaves. Ladle mixture into a 13 x 9 baking dish, cover to edges with mashed potatoes, smoothing with knife. Sprinkle cheddar cheese over top and bake for 15 minutes in a 350° oven or place under broiler until lightly browned.

About Historic Rugby

The Rugby Colony was founded in 1880 by noted English author/social reformer Thomas Hughes. Today, only 20 of the original Victorian buildings still stand. Historic Rugby hosts three major public events each year: the Spring Music & Crafts Festival in May, Historic Rugby Pilgrimage in September and Christmas at Rugby in December.

Sautéed Frog Legs

Tennessee Department of Tourist Development—Nashville

4 Tbsp. BUTTER	FLOUR for dredging
4 pairs FROG LEGS	

Heat butter in a sauté pan. Dredge frogs legs in flour; sauté over medium heat until tender.

Southern Fried Chicken

"The secret is marinating the chicken in buttermilk overnight. There are never any leftovers with this meal!"

Linda Webb—Knoxville

2-3 lbs. CHICKEN PIECES
1-2 cups BUTTERMILK
2 cups SELF-RISING FLOUR
1 tsp. PEPPER
1 tsp. PAPRIKA

1 tsp. ONION POWDER
1/2 tsp. SAGE
1/4 tsp. GARLIC POWDER
COOKING OIL

Wash chicken pieces and pat dry with paper towels. Place chicken in a bowl or zip-lock bag and cover with buttermilk. Refrigerate at least 2-3 hours or overnight. In a bowl, combine flour and seasonings. Dredge each piece of chicken in flour mixture; repeat. In a skillet, heat 1-2 inches of oil. Fry chicken until tender, golden brown and juices run clear; drain on paper towels.

Tennessee Recreation

Tennessee contains all or part of nine national parks, historic sites and recreation areas, including the Great Smoky Mountains National Park, the most visited National Park in the United States.

Baked Country Ham

"Tennessee is well-known for its aged, salted country hams!"

Annie Sue Whited—Lebanon

1 COUNTRY HAM
21 SACCHARIN TABLETS

1 1/2 qts. WATER
BROWN SUGAR

Place ham in a large container and cover with water; let soak several hours or overnight. Preheat oven to 375°. Cut off hock and place ham skin-side-up on aluminum foil in a large roasting pan. Dissolve saccharin tablets in 1 1/2 quarts of water; pour over ham. Bake at 375° until water boils; reduce temperature to 275° and continue baking for 3 1/2-4 hours or until meat thermometer reads 165°. Take out ham and remove skin and fat. Rub ham with brown sugar. Broil for 5 minutes.

Cornbread & Chicken Casserole

"My daughter and I created this dish."

Shirley Woods—Cleveland

5 cups leftover CORNBREAD
1/4 cup finely chopped ONION
1/3 cup chopped CELERY
2 EGGS, beaten

1/4 cup BUTTER or
  MARGARINE, melted
SALT and PEPPER
3 cups HOT CHICKEN BROTH

Preheat oven to 400° and lightly grease an 8 x 8 baking dish. In a mixing bowl, combine finely crumbled cornbread and the next 4 ingredients. Add salt and pepper to taste and stir well. Place 1/2 of the mixture in a baking dish; arrange chicken on top, then spread remaining mixture over chicken. Pour broth evenly over all. Bake for 45 minutes, until lightly browned.

The First Miniature Golf Course

Garnet Carter of Chattanooga invented miniature golf. His first Tom Thumb golf course was built at the Fairyland Inn Hotel on Lookout Mountain in 1926.

Barbecued Chicken

Linda Moulton—Springfield

2 1/2 to 3 lbs. CHICKEN PIECES

Barbecue sauce:
  2 tsp. KETCHUP
  2 tsp. VINEGAR
  2 tsp. BUTTER
  2 tsp. WORCESTERSHIRE
    SAUCE
  2 tsp. LEMON JUICE

4 tsp. WATER
1/2 tsp. GROUND RED
  PEPPER
1 tsp. MUSTARD
1 tsp. PAPRIKA
1 tsp. CHILI POWDER

Wash chicken pieces in cold water and pat dry with paper towels. In a bowl, combine all sauce ingredients. Dip chicken in sauce and place in a heavy aluminum foil package, pouring remaining sauce over top. Seal foil tightly and place in a heavy baking dish or iron skillet. Bake at 500° for 15 minutes, then reduce temperature to 350° and bake for 1 hour and 15 minutes.

Beef Medallions in Cognac Sauce

"This is a favorite dish at our resort."

Chef Karen Valentine—Christopher Place-An Intimate Resort, Newport

2 Tbsp. UNSALTED BUTTER
1/4 cup chopped SHALLOTS
1 tsp. BROWN SUGAR
1 cup LOW SALT CHICKEN
    BROTH
1/2 cup BEEF BROTH

1/2 cup COGNAC
1/4 cup WHIPPING CREAM
2 (4-5 oz. ea.) BEEF
    TENDERLOINS
SALT and PEPPER to taste
CHIVES

Melt 1 tablespoon butter in a heavy saucepan over medium heat. Add shallots and sauté until tender (about 4 minutes). Add brown sugar and stir one minute. Add chicken broth, beef broth and cognac. Simmer until reduced to 1/2 cup (about 20 minutes). Add cream. Sprinkle steaks with salt and pepper and melt remaining butter in skillet over medium-high heat. Add steaks to skillet and cook to desired doneness; transfer to serving plate. Add sauce to skillet and bring to a boil, scraping up any brown bits. Add additional seasoning as desired. Slice steaks and fan out on plates. Spoon sauce over top and garnish with chives.

Easy Chicken Dish

Judy Reaves—Greeneville

1 cup SOUR CREAM
1 can (10.75 oz.) CREAM OF CHICKEN SOUP
1 can (10.75 oz.) CREAM OF MUSHROOM SOUP
8 cups shredded cooked CHICKEN
2 sticks MARGARINE, melted
3 pkgs. (4 oz. ea.) RITZ® CRACKERS, crushed

In a large bowl, combine sour cream, soups and chicken and mix well. Pour mixture into a 13 x 9 pan. In a separate bowl, toss margarine and crackers and spread over top of chicken mixture. Bake at 350° for 30-45 minutes.

White Chicken Chili with Hush Puppy Dumplings

This recipe, by Gaynell Lawson of Maryville, was chosen to represent Tennessee in the 43rd National Chicken Cooking Contest.

National Chicken Council

Chili:
- 1 DRIED ANAHEIM CHILE PEPPER, rehydrated
- 4 boneless, skinless CHICKEN BREASTS, halved
- 3 cans (14.5 oz. ea.) CHICKEN BROTH
- 2 Tbsp. OLIVE OIL
- 3/4 cup finely chopped ONION
- 2 cloves GARLIC, minced
- 1/2 cup chopped GREEN BELL PEPPER
- 1/2 tsp. CUMIN
- 1 Tbsp. CHILI POWDER
- 2 Tbsp. LIME JUICE
- 1 can (19 oz.) CANNELLINI BEANS

Garnish:
- 1/2 cup SOUR CREAM
- 6 Tbsp. SALSA

Remove stem and seeds from chile pepper. Place chicken in a shallow baking dish; add chile pepper and 1 cup chicken broth. Bake in a 350° oven for 30 minutes, turning once. Cut chicken into bite-size pieces; chop chile pepper. In a large saucepan, mix together chicken, chile pepper and remaining chicken broth. Place saucepan over medium heat and bring to a simmer. In a small skillet, place olive oil, onion, garlic, bell pepper, cumin and chili powder; sauté about 3 minutes or until vegetables are tender. Add sautéed mixture to chicken. Add lime juice and cannellini beans; simmer while preparing dumplings. Bring chili to a boil and then carefully drop in dumpling batter (next page) by rounded teaspoons. Cover, reduce heat to simmer and cook 15 minutes without lifting lid. Garnish each serving with a dollop of sour cream and a tablespoon of salsa.

(Continued on next page)

White Chicken Chili with Hush Puppy Dumplings
(Continued from previous page)

Hush Puppy Dumplings

1/4 cup SELF-RISING YELLOW CORNMEAL MIX	1/3 cup BUTTERMILK
	2 Tbsp. chopped PARSLEY
1/4 cup finely chopped ONION	1/2 cup FLOUR

In a bowl, combine all ingredients thoroughly.

Memphis

In 1739, Fort Assumption, the first permanent structure in this area, was built on the bluffs of the Mississippi River. In 1819, Andrew Jackson helped found and name the settlement after a city in Egypt–Memphis, "place of good abode." In 1977, Congress honored W. C. Handy (Father of the Blues) by declaring Memphis "Home of the Blues."

Elvis' Hamburger Steak

Elvis Presley Enterprises, Inc.—Memphis

2 1/2 lbs. GROUND BEEF
1/2 cup chopped ONIONS
1/2 cup chopped BELL PEPPER
1 Tbsp. GARLIC
1 Tbsp. SALT
1 Tbsp. BLACK PEPPER
2 EGGS
3 Tbsp. CRISCO®
2 cans (10.75 oz. ea.) MUSHROOM SOUP

©EPE

Preheat oven to 350°. In a bowl, mix ground beef and all other ingredients except Crisco and mushroom soup. Make into steak-sized patties. Heat Crisco in a skillet, add patties and brown on both sides. Arrange patties in a baking dish and pour mushroom soup over top. Place dish in oven and bake for 1 hour.

Note: This recipe and artwork used by permission Elvis Presley Enterprises, Inc.—www.elvis.com.

Chicken & Dressing Southern-Style

"My grandmother taught me how to make this dressing."

Brenda Kellow—Lebanon

1 BAKING HEN (with GIBLETS) or 2 sm. FRYERS
1 tsp. SALT
1 tsp. coarse ground BLACK
    PEPPER
1 tsp. ONION POWDER
2 1/2 qts. WATER
1 stick MARGARINE, coarsely chopped

Dressing:
    1 pkg. (16 oz.) SELF-RISING CORNBREAD MIX
    4-6 BISCUITS
    2 Tbsp. BACON DRIPPINGS
    1 sm. ONION, diced
    2 stalks CELERY, diced
    1 med. GREEN BELL PEPPER, chopped
    BROTH from cooked chicken
    1 can (12 oz.) EVAPORATED MILK
    2 Tbsp. SAGE
    1/2 tsp. GARLIC POWDER
    3 cups diced cooked CHICKEN

Gravy:
    3 Tbsp. OIL
    1 heaping Tbsp. SELF-RISING FLOUR
    BROTH from cooked chicken
    2 HARD-BOILED EGGS, finely chopped
    SALT and PEPPER
    Finely chopped GIBLETS

Sprinkle chicken with 1/2 teaspoon of salt, 1/2 teaspoon of pepper and 1/2 teaspoon of onion powder and place in a large baking pan. Add giblets, water, margarine and remaining salt, pepper and onion powder. Cover and bake at 375° for 2 hours or until tender. Remove chicken from pan and allow to cool, then debone and dice. Reserve broth and allow to cool; do not

(Continued on next page)

Chicken & Dressing Southern-Style
(Continued from previous page)

skim off chicken fat. Prepare cornbread according to package directions, using 3 eggs in batter and cook in a skillet. In another skillet, heat bacon drippings and sauté onion, celery and bell pepper for 5 minutes. In a bowl, crumble 1/2 of the cornbread and 4-5 biscuits; pour milk and reserved broth, (set aside 1 1/2 cups for gravy) over bread. Add more cornbread or biscuits if needed to make dressing thick.* Stir in onion mixture; add garlic powder and sage and mix well. Cover and refrigerate overnight. Spoon 1/2 of the dressing into a 9 x 9 baking dish. Arrange chicken on top of dressing; spoon remaining dressing over all. Bake at 350° for 45 minutes. In a saucepan, combine oil and flour and cook over medium heat for 1-2 minutes or until smooth. Stir in reserved 1 1/2 cups broth and cook until gravy thickens; remove from heat. Add eggs, giblets, salt and pepper to taste. Spoon gravy over individual servings of chicken and dressing. Serve with **CRANBERRY SAUCE** on the side.

*Dressing may seem too thick, but it will thin when baked.

Quack! Quack!
The Peabody Hotel in Memphis continues a time-honored tradition: Twice daily, a quartet of ducks march to and from the lobby fountain on their own red carpet—to the strains of John Philip Sousa!

Ham & Red-Eye Gravy
"You must have sugar-cured ham to make this right!"

Brenda Burke—Fall Branch

3-4 slices SUGAR-CURED HAM   **1/2 cup HOT WATER**
3 Tbsp. STRONG BLACK COFFEE

In a medium skillet, brown ham slices; remove and place on a serving plate. Drain all but 3 tablespoons of drippings from skillet and heat for 1 minute. Combine coffee with water and stir into drippings. Pour gravy over ham slices and serve.

Crawfish Pie

1 med. ONION	1 can (10.75 oz.) CREAM
3 stalks CELERY	OF MUSHROOM SOUP
6 cloves GARLIC	1 lb. CRAWFISH TAILS
2 Tbsp. BUTTER	5 Tbsp. CORNSTARCH
1 can (12 oz.) EVAPORATED MILK	2 (9-inch) PIE CRUSTS

Preheat oven to 350°. In a large skillet, sauté onion, celery and garlic in butter. Add milk and soup; bring to medium boil. Add crawfish, bring to medium boil again and add cornstarch. Lower heat and cook for another 10 minutes or until mixture is thick. Place one pie crust in pie pan; dot with butter. Add crawfish mixture. Top with second crust, seal edges and vent. Bake at 350° for 20 minutes.

Ribs of Hellspice

"I first offered this seasoning on my website in 1995. Since then, 40% of my sales have come from repeat customers—dozens of whom write to me telling of their fondness for the product."

Eric Ogle—Tennessee Hellspice (www.hellspice.com), Newport

Secret Sauce (sshhh!)
1 cup KETCHUP
1 cup APPLE CIDER VINEGAR
1/2 cup DARK CORN SYRUP or MOLASSES
1/2 cup HONEY
3 Tbsp. TENNESSEE HELLSPICE®
1 Tbsp. SUGAR

4 lbs. PORK BABY BACK RIBS
Generous slathering of SECRET SAUCE

In a saucepan, bring sauce ingredients to a boil over medium-high heat. Cook, stirring with a wire whisk, for 30-45 minutes or until thickened. Cover ribs with sauce. Wrap each rib section in foil, place packets on broiling pan rack and put in a 300° oven. Cook for 2 hours or until meat shrinks back from the bone about 1/2 inch. Remove foil from ribs and slather again with sauce. Cover one half of an outdoor grill with foil; place ribs on the foil and close lid. Slow-cook for 2 hours or until ribs test done and sauce is charred.

Mushroom Meatloaf

Tennessee Department of Agriculture—Nashville

1 1/2 lb. GROUND BEEF
1 lb. GROUND PORK SHOULDER
1 lb. GROUND VEAL
1/3 cup JACK DANIEL'S®
    TENNESSEE WHISKEY
2 tsp. BLACK PEPPER
3 oz. DRIED MUSHROOMS
1 cup minced ONIONS
2 cloves GARLIC, minced

2 Tbsp. BUTTER
1/2 cup soft fresh WHITE
    BREAD CRUMBS
1 EGG, beaten
1/4 cup minced PARSLEY
1 tsp. THYME
3 tsp. SALT
5 strips BACON

Mix together beef, pork, veal, whiskey and black pepper. In a saucepan, pour boiling water over mushrooms to cover and let stand for 20 minutes (reserve water for use in other recipes such as soup, gravies etc.) Drain mushrooms, dry on paper towels and chop into 1/4-inch dice. Add to meat mixture. Preheat oven to 350°. Sauté onions and garlic in butter until limp. Add to meat mixture along with all remaining ingredients except bacon. Mix well. Place in a loaf pan and arrange bacon strips on top. Place in center of oven and bake for one hour. Allow to rest for 20 minutes before cutting into slices.

Serves 8.

Paris & the Eiffel Tower in Tennessee?

Named in honor of the French aid received during the American Revolution, Paris, Tennessee, also erected a 65-foot replica of the Eiffel Tower! During the last full week of April, the World's Biggest Fish Fry serves out more than 12,000 pounds of catfish. And don't miss the catfish races on the courthouse lawn!

Side Dishes

Eggplant Casserole

"As an alternative to cooked and mashed eggplant casseroles, I developed this recipe which features fried eggplant."

Marjorie H. Hoffman—Lebanon

1 lg. EGGPLANT
SALT, PEPPER and SUGAR
1/2 cup WHEAT GERM
COOKING OIL
2 EGGS
1 lg. WHITE ONION, chopped

3-4 med. TOMATOES, chopped
BREAD CRUMBS
2 cups shredded CHEDDAR CHEESE

Wash eggplant, cut off ends and, if desired, peel. Slice eggplant into 1/4-inch thick slices and place in a large mixing bowl. Add salt, pepper and sugar to taste and toss. In a large heavy skillet, heat 1/4-inch cooking oil. In a shallow dish, beat eggs. Add wheat germ to another shallow dish. Using tongs, dip each slice of eggplant into egg; drain slightly and then dredge in wheat germ. Place slices in skillet and fry until golden brown on both sides. Remove and place on paper towels to drain. Lightly grease a casserole dish and arrange layers of eggplant, onion, tomato, bread crumbs and cheese; repeat. Bake at 350° for 30-40 minutes.

Dollywood's®
Fried Green Tomatoes

*"This recipe from Dolly's mother was provided by
Dolly's sister, Willadeene."*

Pete Owens, Director of Marketing—Dollywood, Pigeon Forge

SALT and PEPPER　　　　　**FLOUR**
Sliced GREEN TOMATOES　　**BACON DRIPPINGS**
Beaten EGGS

Salt and pepper tomato slices to taste, dip in egg and dredge in flour. In a skillet, heat bacon drippings over medium-high heat and fry tomato slices until brown on both sides.

Dolly Parton's Dollywood

(http://www.dollywood.com)
*This unique entertainment park at the foothills of the
Smokies has many attractions—including:*

Places to Eat:
- *Aunt Granny's Restaurant*
- *Granny Ogle's Ham 'n' Beans*
- *Spotlight Bakery*

Themed Rides:
- *Daredevil Falls*
- *Dolly's Demolition Derby*
- *Thunder Road*

Places to Shop:
- *Butterfly Emporium*
- *Dolly's Dressing Room*
- *Sweet Dreams Candy Shop*
- *Cas Walker's General Store*
- *Old Flames Candle Shop*
- *Uncle Bill's Guitar Shop*

Fried
Pumpkin Blossoms

Kathy Stacy—Fall Branch

Pick large **PUMPKIN BLOSSOMS** and wash carefully. Coat blossoms on both sides with **CORNMEAL**. In a heavy skillet, heat **BACON DRIPPINGS** and fry blossoms over medium heat until golden brown and crisp. Serve hot.

Sweet Potato Casserole

Shirley A. Viar—Dyersburg

3 cups cooked and mashed
    SWEET POTATOES
1/3 cup MILK
1/2 cup MARGARINE

1 cup SUGAR
2 EGGS, beaten
1 tsp. VANILLA

Topping:
    1 cup packed LIGHT BROWN
        SUGAR
    1/2 cup ALL-PURPOSE FLOUR

    1/3 cup MARGARINE, melted
    1 cup chopped NUTS

In a bowl, combine sweet potatoes, milk, margarine, sugar, eggs and vanilla and mix well. Spoon into a buttered 2-quart casserole dish. In a bowl, combine topping ingredients; sprinkle evenly on casserole. Bake for 25-30 minutes at 350°.

Knoxville

Originally the site of James White's Fort, this city was the territorial capital from 1792-1796 and the state capital from 1796-1811, and again in 1817. Take a free trolley ride to visit the Blount Mansion, the Knoxville Museum of Art and the Women's Basketball Hall of Fame.

Slow-Baked Tennessee Tomatoes

Tennessee Department of Agriculture—Nashville

6 lg. TOMATOES, cut in half
    horizontally
6 tsp. OLIVE OIL
SALT and PEPPER

3 cloves GARLIC, minced
1/3 cup crumbled GOAT
    CHEESE
3 Tbsp. chopped BASIL

Preheat oven to 325°. Place tomatoes on a baking sheet, cut-sides up. Drizzle with oil and sprinkle with salt and pepper to taste. Bake 2-3 hours or until the tomatoes collapse and begin to caramelize. Sprinkle with garlic about halfway through baking and goat cheese during last five minutes. Sprinkle with basil just before serving.

Squash Dressing Casserole

"This is an excellent way to use fresh squash!"

Linda Moulton—Springfield

1/2 stick BUTTER
1 sm. ONION, chopped
2 cups cubed and cooked YELLOW SQUASH, well drained
2 cups DAY-OLD CORNBREAD CRUMBS
1 EGG, lightly beaten
1 can (10.75 oz.) CREAM OF MUSHROOM SOUP, undiluted
1 cup MILK
SALT and PEPPER

In a skillet, melt butter and sauté onion until translucent. In a bowl, combine squash, onion and remaining ingredients and mix lightly. Pour mixture into a greased casserole dish. Bake at 350° for 40-50 minutes until set and brown on top.

Nashville

Founded in 1779, this city was first named Fort Nashborough. In 1784 it was renamed Nashville and permanently established as the capital city of Tennessee in 1843. This city ranks, in area, as one of the nation's largest. Some places to visit include: Country Music Hall of Fame & Museum; Ernest Tubb Record Shop in Music Valley Village; Grand Ole Opry Museum; Willie Nelson Museum. You can also schedule a cruise on the world's largest showboat, the General Jackson.

Escalloped Spoon Corn

Anita Urban—Moscow

1 stick MARGARINE, melted
1 can (14.75 oz.) CREAM STYLE CORN
1 can (15.25 oz.) WHOLE KERNEL CORN, with liquid
2 EGGS, beaten
1 cup SOUR CREAM
1 box (8.5 oz.) JIFFY® CORN MUFFIN MIX

In a mixing bowl, combine all ingredients and mix well. Pour mixture into a buttered 13 x 9 casserole dish. Bake at 350° for 40 minutes.

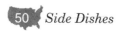

Tennessee Vegetable Fritters

"This is the best of my mother's okra recipes. It is delicious!"

Druceil K. Henry—Crossville

2 cups thinly sliced OKRA
3/4 cup finely chopped GREEN
   TOMATO
1/2 cup thinly sliced GREEN
   ONIONS
1/2 cup CORNMEAL MIX

2 EGGS, beaten
4 Tbsp. MILK or CREAM
1/2 tsp. SALT
1 tsp. TABASCO® (optional)
OIL for frying

In a bowl, combine all ingredients, except oil, and mix well. In a heavy skillet, heat 1/2-inch oil to 375°. Carefully drop batter in oil by tablespoon. Cook for 2-3 minutes until edges start to brown, turn and brown other side; drain on paper towels.

Sweet Potato Soufflé

This recipe is from "Home and Away: A University Brings Food to the Table—Recipes and Remembrances from East Tennessee State University."

Fred Sauceman—East Tennessee State University, Johnson City

2 lbs. SWEET POTATOES
1 1/2 cups SUGAR
2 EGGS, beaten
3/4 stick BUTTER, softened

1 tsp. freshly grated NUTMEG
1 tsp. CINNAMON
1 cup MILK

Topping:
1/2 cup BROWN SUGAR
1 cup chopped PECANS

3/4 cup crushed CORN FLAKES
3/4 stick BUTTER

Boil sweet potatoes in skins until tender. Cool, peel and chunk, then purée in food processor until smooth. Add remaining ingredients and process until well-blended. Pour into a greased casserole dish and bake, uncovered, at 350° for 35-40 minutes or until almost set. In a bowl, combine topping ingredients; sprinkle over potatoes. Bake 15 minutes longer.

Hush Puppies for Two

"You know how this dish got its name? Some hunters' dogs were barking around the supper table. One hunter threw down some of this food and said, 'Hush Puppies!' That's the story, anyway!"

Ella D. Loveday—Crossville

1/2 cup SELF-RISING CORNMEAL	1 EGG, beaten
3/4 Tbsp. SELF-RISING FLOUR	1/4 cup BUTTERMILK
1 Tbsp. chopped ONION	COOKING OIL

In a mixing bowl, combine cornmeal and flour; add onion, egg and buttermilk and mix well. Set batter aside to thicken. In a deep kettle, heat oil and carefully drop tablespoons of batter into hot oil. Adjust temperature to keep oil from getting too hot, so Hush Puppies won't brown too quickly before the center is done. Usually, Hush Puppies will float when they need to be turned over. Cook until light to medium brown.

The Appalachian & Cumberland Trails

The Appalachian Trail in the Great Smoky Mountains of eastern Tennessee can be accessed from many points along its route. The Cumberland Trail State Park, created in 1998, is a 282-mile route from Chattanooga to Cumberland Gap National Historical Park on the northeastern border with Kentucky.

Fried Okra

Tennessee Department of Tourist Development—Nashville

1 lb. OKRA PODS, stem ends cut off	SALT and PEPPER
COLD WATER	COOKING OIL
CORNMEAL	

Slice pods into 1/2-inch slices. Sprinkle with salt and cover with very cold water. Refrigerate for about an hour. Drain. Roll slices in cornmeal that has been seasoned with salt and pepper, until well-coated. Fry in 1/2-inch deep oil until browned and crisp. Drain on paper towels. Serve hot.

Mama's Baked Beans

"This is a treasured recipe from my mother, Jean Botts."

Becky Arnott—Kingsport

1 can (16 oz.) PORK AND BEANS
2 Tbsp. KETCHUP
1 tsp. PREPARED MUSTARD

1/3 cup MAPLE SYRUP
1 sm. ONION, peeled

In a medium bowl, combine beans, ketchup, mustard and syrup and mix well. Pour into casserole dish and place onion in center (make a slit in onion to allow juices to flavor dish). Bake uncovered at 375° for 30 minutes.

Gatlinburg

Gatlinburg sits just 2 miles north of the entrance to the Great Smoky Mountains National Park. Attractions include the Aerial Tramway, The Great Smoky Arts and Crafts Community, Christus Gardens, Guinness World Records Museum, Ober Gatlinburg and Ripley's Aquarium of the Smokies.

Southern Fried Corn

"Fried corn in the South is a staple during the growing season. My grandmother taught me how to make it. Everyone in the South anticipates the first 'roasting ears' to be harvested."

Brenda Kellow—Lebanon

8 ears SILVER QUEEN
**   SWEET CORN**
2 Tbsp. BACON DRIPPINGS
2 cups WATER

1/2 tsp. SALT
1/8 tsp. coarse ground
**   BLACK PEPPER**

Remove husks and silks from corn and wash ears thoroughly. In a large rimmed bowl, cut kernels from cobs, then scrape cobs to get the starchy juices that will thicken the corn while cooking. In a large skillet, heat bacon drippings and add corn, water, salt and pepper. Cook over medium heat until mixture thickens and corn is tender.

Stuffed Pumpkin

Donna Ybarra—Four Season's Market, Lebanon

1 (8- to10-inch) PUMPKIN	1 tsp. CINNAMON
1 cup CRANBERRIES	1/4 tsp. CLOVES
1/2 cup DATES	1/4 tsp. ALLSPICE
1/3 cup WALNUTS	1/4 tsp. NUTMEG
1 cup chopped TART APPLES	1 tsp. grated LEMON RIND
1/4 cup BROWN SUGAR	1 Tbsp. grated ORANGE RIND

Cut top off the pumpkin and set aside. Scoop out inside. Combine all stuffing ingredients and fill pumpkin. Bake, without top, for 45 minutes at 350°. Place top on pumpkin and continue baking for 30 minutes. Serve warm.

The Parthenon at Nashville

Built for the 1897 Tennessee Centennial, this is a full-size replica—the world's only reproduction of the ancient temple at Athens, Greece. It houses many sculptures, including a 42-foot-high sculpture of Athena, the goddess of wisdom.

Tipsy Sweet Potatoes

Jack Daniel's Distillery (www.jackdaniels.com)—Lynchburg

4 lg. SWEET POTATOES
1/4 cup BUTTER
3/4 cup packed LIGHT BROWN SUGAR
1/8 tsp. SALT
1/4 cup JACK DANIEL'S® TENNESSEE WHISKEY
1/2 cup chopped PECANS, lightly toasted

Boil sweet potatoes until tender, about 35 minutes; cool. Peel potatoes and place in a mixing bowl. Mash with butter, then stir in sugar, salt and whiskey. In a buttered 2-quart casserole dish, spread half of the potatoes and sprinkle with half of the pecans. Repeat layers. Bake at 325° for 30 minutes.

Chocolate Almond Muffins

*"We love to create new dishes to tempt our guests' palates.
This is a favorite."*

Judy & Robert Hotchkiss—Prospect Hill Bed & Breakfast Inn,
Mountain City

1/3 cup SUGAR
4 Tbsp. UNSALTED BUTTER
 or MARGARINE
2 EGGS
1 tsp. VANILLA EXTRACT
1 tsp. ALMOND EXTRACT
1 1/2 cups ALL-PURPOSE FLOUR

1/2 cup COCOA POWDER
3 tsp. BAKING POWDER
1/4 tsp. SALT
3/4 cup MILK
3/4 cup SEMI-SWEET or
 MINI-CHIP CHOCOLATES

In a large bowl, melt butter and sugar together in a microwave (approximately 30 seconds). Add eggs and mix thoroughly. Stir in extracts. Combine dry ingredients in a sifter and sift into wet mixture. Stir in milk until just mixed. Stir in chocolate chips. Add 1/4 cup batter to sprayed (flavorless, nonstick spray) muffin cups. Bake at 425° for 10-15 minutes or until muffins test done. Do not overcook. Cool before removing from pan.

Oatmeal Banana Nut Bread

"This is so good!"

Dorothy H. Bowling—Knoxville

1/2 cup SHORTENING
1 cup SUGAR
2 EGGS
1 cup mashed BANANAS
1 1/2 cups FLOUR
1 tsp. BAKING SODA
1/4 tsp. SALT
1/2 cup QUICK-COOKING OATS
3/4 cup chopped PECANS
1 tsp. VANILLA

In a large bowl, cream together shortening and sugar; add eggs, one at a time, blending well after each addition. Stir in bananas and mix well. In another bowl, sift together flour, baking soda and salt; add alternately with oats to creamed mixture. Stir in pecans and vanilla. Pour batter into a greased 9 x 5 loaf pan. Bake at 350° for 50-55 minutes or until a toothpick inserted in the middle comes out clean.

Apple Bread

"We sell this bread in small loaves at our farm market. It goes like 'hot cakes'!"

Cecileia Shultz—Shultz Farm Foods, Athens

3 EGGS
2 cups SUGAR
1 cup VEGETABLE OIL
2 cups grated APPLES
3 tsp. VANILLA

3 cups FLOUR
1 tsp. BAKING SODA
1/4 tsp. BAKING POWDER
1 tsp. SALT
3 tsp. CINNAMON

Preheat oven to 350°. In a bowl, beat eggs; mix in sugar, oil, apples and vanilla. In another bowl, combine dry ingredients, then add to apple mixture. Blend. Pour batter into two 9 x 5 loaf pans. Bake for 1 hour.

Cornlight Bread
"This is a wonderful Southern recipe!"

Norma Taylor—Casey Jones Home & Railroad Museum, Jackson

2 cups SELF-RISING CORNMEAL
1 cup SELF-RISING FLOUR
3/4 cup SUGAR
2 cups BUTTERMILK
3 Tbsp. COOKING OIL

In a bowl, mix cornmeal, flour and sugar. Add buttermilk and oil and blend well. Pour batter into a greased loaf pan or tube pan. Bake at 350° for 45 minutes. Remove from pan and cool before slicing.

Note: This recipe can also be used for muffins. Pour batter into a greased muffin tin and bake at 350° for 20-25 minutes.

The Story of Casey Jones

Raised in the little town of Cayce, Kentucky, where he got his nickname, Casey Jones became an engineer on the Illinois Central Railroad, married in 1886 and made Jackson his home. In April of 1900, despite his best efforts to stop his engine, he was killed when the train hit stalled cars on the track near Vaughan, Mississippi. Every passenger on his train was saved because of his heroic actions. Visit the Historic Casey Jones Home and Railroad Museum in Jackson to learn more of this famous American hero.

The Ballad of Casey Jones

Come all you rounders if you want to hear
A story about a brave engineer.
Casey Jones was the rounder's name
On a six-eight wheeler boys he rode to fame.
Chorus:
Casey Jones mounted to the cabin,
Casey Jones with his orders in his hand.
Casey Jones mounted to the cabin
And he took his farewell trip to the promised land.

Chocolate Banana Nut Bread

"This is one of 12 recipes chosen for our 'Year 2000' bank calendar. It is also a favorite in our church cookbook."

Imogene M. Engle—Home Federal Bank, Knoxville

1 tsp. BAKING SODA	2 cups ALL-PURPOSE FLOUR
1/4 cup WARM WATER	1/3 cup UNSWEETENED
12 Tbsp. BUTTER	COCOA POWDER
1 1/3 cup SUGAR	1 tsp. VANILLA
2 lg. EGGS	1 cup chopped PECANS
3 BANANAS, mashed	or WALNUTS

Preheat oven to 350°. Grease and flour a 9 x 5 loaf pan; set aside. In a small bowl, combine baking soda and warm water. In another bowl, beat together butter and sugar until light and fluffy. Add eggs, one at a time, beating 30 seconds after each addition. Beat in bananas. With mixer on low speed, gradually add flour, cocoa powder, baking soda mixture and vanilla. Beat until just blended. Hand stir in nuts. Pour mixture into loaf pan and bake for 1 hour or until tests done. Cool at least 5 minutes before removing from pan.

Miss Daisy's Pumpkin Bread

Daisy King for Brooks Parker—East Park Inn, An Urban Bed & Breakfast, Nashville

4 cups SUGAR	2 tsp. CINNAMON
1 can (29 oz.) PUMPKIN	2 tsp. ground CLOVES
3 EGGS	2 cups chopped WALNUTS
1 cup VEGETABLE OIL	2 cups chopped DATES
5 cups FLOUR	

Preheat oven to 350°. In a large bowl, combine the first 4 ingredients. Gently stir in dry ingredients just until moist. Fold in nuts and dates until evenly distributed. Pour batter into two greased and floured loaf pans. Bake for 1 hour or until toothpick inserted in center comes out clean.

Banana Nut Bread

"This recipe came from my neighbor, Mrs. Tom Sterk."

Anita Urban—Moscow

1/2 cup MARGARINE
1 cup SUGAR
1 EGG, beaten
3/4 tsp. BAKING SODA
1 1/2 cups FLOUR

1 Tbsp. BAKING POWDER
1/2 tsp. SALT
3 BANANAS, mashed
1/2 cup chopped NUTS

In a large bowl, cream together margarine and sugar. Stir in remaining ingredients and mix well. Pour mixture into a greased loaf pan. Bake at 350° for 50-60 minutes or until a toothpick inserted in the center comes out clean.

 **Natchez Trace Parkway**

Beginning just below Nashville, this 444-mile route to Natchez, Mississippi, began as an Indian pathway. The Parkway angles southwest about 100 miles, crossing into Alabama at Cypress Inn. Whether biking, hiking or touring in your car, you will find the parkway a wondrous adventure.

Hot Gingerbread

"My grandma and my mother always kept molasses and ginger on hand and saved coffee for this bread."

Druceil K. Henry—Crossville

1/2 cup BUTTER
1/2 cup STRONG HOT COFFEE
2 EGGS, beaten
1/2 cup SUGAR

1/2 cup MOLASSES
1 1/2 cups FLOUR
1 tsp. GINGER
2 tsp. BAKING POWDER

In a bowl, melt butter in hot coffee. In a another bowl, combine eggs, sugar and molasses. Combine mixtures. Sift flour, ginger and baking powder into mixture and mix to form a soft dough. Spread batter 1/2-inch thick on a greased and floured baking pan. Bake at 350° for 25 minutes.

Holiday Finger Biscuits

"This recipe was created for young children."

Tena Huckleby—Greeneville

2 cups SELF-RISING FLOUR
2 cups CAKE FLOUR (not self-rising)
1 tsp. CINNAMON
8 Tbsp. UNSALTED BUTTER, chilled
1 1/4-1 1/2 cups COLD MILK
1/4 cup diced PINEAPPLE, drained
1/4 cup diced RED CHERRIES
1/4 cup diced GREEN CHERRIES
1/4 cup diced ORANGES
1/4 cup diced CRANBERRIES

Orange Butter:
  1 1/2 cups BUTTER, softened
  6 Tbsp. grated ORANGE PEEL

Preheat oven to 425°. In a bowl, combine both flours and cinnamon. With a pastry blender, cut in butter until mixture forms coarse crumbs. Add milk and toss gently with a fork, using only enough milk to make dough moist, not wet. Fold in fruit. Turn dough out onto a floured surface and gently knead 2-3 times. Roll dough into a 1/2-inch thick rectangle and cut into 24 (1-inch) squares. Place squares on a greased baking sheet, spacing at least 1/8-inch apart. Bake 10-14 minutes until golden brown. Mix together butter and orange peel in small bowl. Serve biscuits warm with **Orange Butter** on the side.

The Battle of Shiloh

Shiloh National Military Park, just southwest of Savannah, preserves the site of the first major Western battle of the Civil War. In 1862 on April 6th and 7th, the Confederate Army, under Generals Albert Johnson and P.G.T. Beauregard and the Union army, led by General Ulysses S. Grant, waged a battle that left almost 24,000 casualties. The victory went to the Union Army as the Confederates retreated into Mississippi.

Cracklin' Bread

"My mother baked this in a 'baker'—an iron pot that was placed in the fireplace with hot coals under it and on the lid. I still have the baker we used."

Mae Burke—Fall Branch

2 cups CORNMEAL
1 cup BUTTERMILK
1/2 tsp. BAKING SODA

1/2 tsp. SALT
1 cup CRACKLIN'S

In a bowl, combine cornmeal, buttermilk, baking soda and salt; stir in cracklin's. Form mixture into oblong cakes and place on a greased baking pan. Bake at 450° for 30 minutes.

Cracklin's
Cracklin's are crunchy pieces of pork or poultry fat which remain after the fat has been rendered.

Indian Bean Bread

Glenda Ezell—Lawrence County Chamber of Commerce,
Lawrenceburg

4 cups CORNMEAL
2 cups cooked BEANS, drained

2 cups HOT WATER
1/2 tsp. BAKING SODA

In a bowl, combine cornmeal and beans. Make a hole in the center of dough, add water and baking soda; mix together. Form mixture into balls and drop into a pot of boiling water. Cook about 45 minutes until done.

Davy Crockett
Although not actually "born on a mountaintop" (he was born in a log cabin on the banks of Limestone Creek near Greeneville), this colorful scout and frontiersman served Tennessee in Congress from 1827-1831 and then again from 1833-1835. In Lawrenceburg, be sure to visit the Crockett Museum located in David Crockett State Park.

Baking Powder Buttermilk Biscuits

"I learned how to make biscuits from my mother, Eunice Buttram Daves, and from my grandmother, Bertie Buttram. My biscuits often won prizes in the Cumberland County Fair when I was in the 4-H Club at Homestead Schools."

Ella D. Loveday—Crossville

1 cup BUTTERMILK	3 tsp. BAKING POWDER
2 cups sifted ALL-PURPOSE FLOUR	1/2 tsp. SALT
	1/3 cup SHORTENING

Preheat oven to 450°. Pour buttermilk into a cup and let sit. In a bowl, combine flour, baking powder and salt. Cut in shortening until mixture forms coarse crumbs; add buttermilk and stir until flour mixture is moist. Turn dough out onto a floured surface and knead until just mixed. Pat out into a rectangle 1/2-inch thick. Dip biscuit cutter into flour, then cut out biscuits and place them on an ungreased baking sheet. Bake for 12-15 minutes.

Gritted Bread

"This bread has been a family favorite for over 50 years. My mother, Mamie Love, often made this for church dinners. I serve this bread when I have dinner guests–everyone loves it!"

Debra Kay Evans—Erwin

12 ears CORN	Pinch of BAKING POWDER
2 EGGS, beaten	1 Tbsp. SUGAR
1 cup FLOUR	1 cup BUTTERMILK
Pinch of SALT	1/4 cup SHORTENING

Preheat oven to 350°. Grate corn from cobs with a "gritter" (grater), into a bowl. In another bowl, combine all ingredients and mix well; stir in corn. Pour batter into a loaf pan and bake for 25 minutes. Serve hot.

Broccoli Cornbread

"This quick and easy-to-make bread became a family favorite many years ago!"

Debbie Bedingfield—Parsons

1 box (8.5 oz) JIFFY® CORN MUFFIN MIX
4 EGGS, beaten
1 pkg. (10 oz.) frozen BROCCOLI, thawed and drained
1 stick BUTTER, melted

In a bowl, combine muffin mix, eggs and broccoli and mix well. Pour mixture into a greased iron skillet. Drizzle butter over top of batter. Bake at 350° for 25-30 minutes or until tests done.

Fort Donelson National Battlefield

In February of 1862, Confederate army troops, retreating from the advance of Union General Ulysses S. Grant, sought refuge in Fort Donelson. When surrounded by Grant's troops, approximately 13,000 men surrendered and became prisoners of war. This was the North's first major victory. Grant became known as "Unconditional Surrender" Grant.

Fried Cornbread Cakes

"This is a recipe of my mother's that I still love to make."

Becky Arnott—Kingsport

1 EGG, beaten
1/4 cup VEGETABLE OIL
1 Tbsp. SUGAR
MILK

2 cups THREE RIVERS®
SELF-RISING CORN-
MEAL MIX

In a 1-cup measuring cup, combine egg, oil and sugar and finish filling with milk. Pour into a bowl; add cornmeal mix and stir well. Spoon mixture, 2 tablespoons at a time, onto a hot, lightly greased griddle; fry until golden brown on both sides.

Holiday Nut Bread

"This festive-looking bread has wonderful taste and texture!"

Jo Ann Vaughn—Von Bryan Mountaintop Inn, Sevierville

2 1/2 cups FLOUR
1 tsp. BAKING SODA
1 Tbsp. BAKING POWDER
1 1/2 tsp. SALT
1 cup SUGAR
1/3 cup VEGETABLE OIL
2 EGGS

3/4 cup SOUR MILK
1 cup mashed BANANAS
1/2 cup peeled and finely
    chopped APPLE
1 cup chopped MARASCHINO
    CHERRIES
1 cup chopped NUTS

Preheat oven to 350°. In a bowl, combine flour, baking soda, baking powder and salt. In another bowl, combine sugar, oil and eggs; mix well. Add flour mixture alternately with milk and bananas, mixing well after each addition. Stir in apples, cherries and nuts. Pour batter into a greased loaf pan and bake for 1 hour or until toothpick inserted in center comes out clean. Cool for 10 minutes and then remove to a wire rack.

Cinnamon Muffins

*"When we opened our Inn, my mother gave me this
recipe that she had saved for years."*

Judy & Robert Hotchkiss—Prospect Hill Bed & Breakfast Inn,
Mountain City

1/2 cup BUTTER, softened
1 cup SUGAR
2 EGGS
1 1/2 cups ALL-PURPOSE FLOUR
2 tsp. BAKING POWDER

Pinch of SALT
1 Tbsp. CINNAMON
1/2 tsp. ALLSPICE
1/2 cup MILK

Preheat oven to 350°. In a bowl, melt butter and sugar together in a microwave (approximately 30 seconds). Beat in eggs. In another bowl, sift together flour, baking powder, salt, cinnamon and allspice. Stir dry ingredients into wet mixture, alternating with milk. Pour batter into greased muffin cups 1/2 to 2/3 full. Do not overfill. Bake for about 15 minutes or until muffins test done. Cool before removing from pan.

Desserts

Tennessee Apple Cake

"We have a dwarf apple tree 'Pick Your Own' orchard as a retirement income/hobby. This cake recipe was developed to showcase our prize Royal Gala apples and to introduce guests and customers to a delicious way of using these wonderful apples for cooking."

Norma M. Weeks—Jackson Ridge Orchard & Apple Cottage, Dandridge

1 cup CANOLA OIL
1 1/2 cups SUGAR
3 EGGS
2 cups ALL-PURPOSE FLOUR
1 tsp. BAKING SODA
Dash of SALT

1 tsp. CINNAMON
1/2 tsp. NUTMEG
1 tsp. PUMPKIN PIE SPICE
5 cups sliced or chopped
   ROYAL GALA APPLES
Chopped PECANS

Cinnamon Sugar Topping:
  2 Tbsp. SUGAR
  1/2 tsp. CINNAMON

Preheat oven to 350°. In a mixing bowl, combine oil and sugar; add eggs, one at a time, beating well after each addition. In another bowl, sift flour with baking soda, salt and spices. Combine mixtures and mix well. Gently fold in apples and pecans. Pour batter into a greased 13 x 9 pan. Bake for 1 hour. To prepare topping: In a small bowl, mix sugar and cinnamon together; sprinkle over top of cake while still hot.

Civil War Egg Custard

"This recipe has been handed down in my family from the days of the Civil War! My grandfather, C. M. Bowlin, was a teacher and merchant in Kingsport for over fifty years."

Ann Goode Cooper—Kingsport

4 EGGS, beaten
8 Tbsp. SUGAR
3 cups MILK
1 tsp. VANILLA

Dash of SALT
NUTMEG
1 (9-inch) unbaked PIE
SHELL

Preheat oven to 450°. In a bowl, combine eggs, sugar, milk and vanilla; mix well. Pour mixture into pie shell. Sprinkle top with desired amount of nutmeg. Bake for 10 minutes; reduce temperature to 350° and continue to bake until custard is set and slightly brown. Test for doneness.

The Buckle on the Bible Belt?

The printing industry, especially the production of Bibles, is of major importance in Nashville. Because of its strong religious ties, Nashville has been referred to as "the buckle on the Bible Belt."

Buttermilk Coconut Pie

Barbara Stagg—Historic Rugby Visitor Center, Rugby

1/4 cup BUTTER or MARGARINE
1 cup SUGAR
2 Tbsp. ALL-PURPOSE FLOUR
Dash of SALT
4 EGGS, lightly beaten

1 cup BUTTERMILK
2 tsp. VANILLA
1 cup grated COCONUT
1 (9-inch) unbaked PIE
SHELL

Melt butter in a saucepan. Remove pan from heat and stir in sugar, flour and salt. Add eggs, buttermilk and vanilla and stir until well-blended. Stir in coconut. Pour batter into pie shell and bake at 350° for 45 minutes or until set and lightly browned.

Tennessee Apple Pie

"Former Governor Lamar Alexander won third place in a pie-baking contest with this recipe."

Dolores Y. Stevens—Knoxville

2 1/2 cups ALL-PURPOSE FLOUR
1/2 tsp. SALT
3/4 cup SHORTENING
6 Tbsp. COLD WATER
1 EGG WHITE, slightly beaten

Filling:
    6 cups (2 lbs.) peeled, thinly sliced
        TART APPLES
    2/3 cup SUGAR
    1/4 cup packed BROWN SUGAR
    1/2 cup ORANGE JUICE
    1/4 tsp. NUTMEG
    1/4 tsp. CINNAMON
    2 Tbsp. BUTTER or MARGARINE

In a bowl, combine flour and salt. With pastry blender or 2 knives used scissor-fashion, cut in shortening until mixture resembles coarse crumbs. Sprinkle with water and stir until mixture is moist and holds together when pressed between hands. Shape pastry into a ball; wrap and chill for 30 minutes. Divide dough into 2 pieces, one slightly larger than the other. On a lightly floured surface, roll out larger piece into an 11-inch circle. Lightly fold the circle into quarters and transfer to a pie plate. Unfold and line pie plate, trimming edge to a 1-inch overhang; brush pastry with 1/2 of the egg white. Preheat oven to 425°. To prepare filling: In a saucepan, combine apples, sugars, orange juice, nutmeg and cinnamon and mix well. Cook for 10 minutes, then remove apple slices with a slotted spoon and set them aside. Boil liquid until it is reduced to 3/4 cup. Spoon apples and liquid into pie shell and dot with butter. Roll out remaining pastry into a 9-inch circle. Cut into ten 1/2-inch wide strips. Weave strips in a lattice pattern over filling and flute edges. Brush strips with remaining egg white and sprinkle lightly with sugar. Bake 40-45 minutes.

Cherry Wink Cookies

*"This popular recipe of the mid-1950s is from
the family recipes of Marie Rafferty."*

Mrs. Waylon Jennings (Jessi Colter)—Brentwood

2 cups FLOUR
1 tsp. BAKING POWDER
1/2 tsp. BAKING SODA
1/2 tsp. SALT
2/3 cup SHORTENING
1 cup SUGAR
2 EGGS, lightly beaten
3 Tbsp. CREAM

1 tsp. VANILLA
1 cup chopped PECANS
1 cup chopped DATES
2 cups crushed
    CORN FLAKES
MARASCHINO CHERRIES,
    halved

In a bowl, sift together flour, baking powder, baking soda and salt. In another bowl, cream shortening and sugar together; blend in eggs, cream and vanilla. Stir in dry ingredients and mix well. Stir in pecans and dates. Measure a level tablespoon of dough and roll it into a ball; roll ball in cornflakes. Place half of a cherry on top. Place cookies on a greased cookie sheet and bake at 375° for 10-12 minutes.

Makes 8 dozen cookies.

Old-Fashioned Tea Cakes

"Our neighbor, Gladys Griffith, was one of my favorite people when I was growing up. She made these tea cakes and kept them in her pie safe so that we could have them when we visited."

Jo Smith—Wilson County Promotions, Inc., Lebanon

1/2 cup BUTTER
1 cup SUGAR
1 EGG, lightly beaten

1/4 cup MILK
1 tsp. VANILLA
3 cups SELF-RISING FLOUR

In a bowl, cream together butter and sugar; add egg, milk and vanilla. Stir in flour and mix well. Roll out dough on a floured surface until very thin; cut with cookie or biscuit cutter and place on a baking sheet. Bake at 325° for 12-15 minutes or until lightly browned.

Custard Crunch Mince Pie

"We wanted a mincemeat pie that did not include suet, so when I found this one, over 50 years ago, it soon became a favorite."

Imogene M. Engle—Knoxville

1 cup SUGAR	1/4 cup BUTTER, melted
2 Tbsp. FLOUR	1 cup HOMEMADE MINCEMEAT
1/8 tsp. SALT	1/2 cup chopped WALNUTS
3 EGGS, lightly beaten	1 (9-inch) unbaked PIE SHELL

In a bowl, combine sugar, flour and salt; add to eggs. Mix in butter, mincemeat and walnuts. Pour batter into pie shell and bake for 15 minutes at 400°. Reduce heat to 325° and continue baking for 30 minutes.

Homemade Mincemeat

1 pkg. (15 oz.) RAISINS	1 lb. BROWN SUGAR
1 cup dried APRICOTS	1 1/2 tsp. CINNAMON
1 cup pitted PRUNES	1/2 tsp. NUTMEG
1 cup dried FIGS	1/2 tsp. CLOVES
2 lbs. TART APPLES, cored	1/2 tsp. GINGER
2 lbs. PEARS, cored	1 1/2 cups chopped WALNUTS
1 lg. SEEDLESS ORANGE	1 cup BOURBON, RUM or
1 unpeeled, seeded LEMON	BRANDY

Grind fruit in order given, using coarse blade of a food chopper. Stir in remaining ingredients. Spoon mixture into three sterilized quart jars and seal. Store in a cool dry place or refrigerate.

About Tennessee's Name

Tennessee is nicknamed the Volunteer State because of its outstanding military traditions (particularly during the War of 1812). This state's name probably comes from "Tanasie" (or "Tanesi"), the name of a Cherokee village in the region. It is also sometimes called the "Big Bend State," as the Indian name for the Tennessee River is "The river with the big bend."

Best Red Velvet Cake

Carmela Peterson—Erwin

2 1/2 cups SELF-RISING FLOUR
1 cup BUTTERMILK
1 1/2 cups VEGETABLE OIL
1 tsp. BAKING SODA
2 bottles (1 oz. ea.) RED FOOD
  COLORING

1 1/2 cups SUGAR
1 tsp. COCOA POWDER
1 tsp. VINEGAR
2 EGGS, beaten
Chopped PECANS

Preheat oven to 350°. In a large bowl, combine all ingredients, except pecans, and blend with electric mixer. Spray three 9-inch cake pans with non-stick cooking spray. Pour batter equally into pans and bake for 20 minutes. Cakes are done when a toothpick inserted in the center comes out clean. Cool cakes in pans on wire rack for 10 minutes, then remove cakes from pans and place on rack to cool completely. Spread *Powdered Sugar Frosting* between layers, then frost top and sides. Sprinkle pecans on top. Refrigerate at least 1 hour before serving.

Powdered Sugar Frosting

8 oz. CREAM CHEESE
1 1/2 sticks BUTTER

1 box (1 lb.) POWDERED
  SUGAR

Combine cream cheese, butter and powdered sugar in a bowl. Beat until fluffy.

Chattanooga

This city's name comes from Creek Indian language that means "rock coming to a point," referring to 2,126-foot-high Lookout Mountain just south of town. The Chickamauga and Chattanooga National Military Park preserves much of the historic area on which the Civil War battles of Lookout Mountain, Chickamauga and Missionary Ridge were fought. Other places to see include: the Chattanooga Choo Choo, the Tennessee Aquarium and Ruby Falls-Lookout Mountain Caverns (ride the Lookout Mountain Incline Railway—one of the steepest in the world!)

Blackberry Jam Cake

"This recipe has been passed down for many generations."

Mrs. Robert T. De Marcus—Knoxville

6 Tbsp. BUTTERMILK
2 tsp. BAKING SODA
2 cups SUGAR
1/2 lb. BUTTER
6 EGGS, beaten
2 tsp. CINNAMON
2 tsp. NUTMEG
2 tsp. CLOVES

2 tsp. ALLSPICE
4 cups FLOUR
2 cups SEEDLESS
    BLACKBERRY JAM
1 lb. RAISINS
1 cup PECANS
1 cup ENGLISH WALNUTS

Combine buttermilk and baking soda and set aside. In a bowl, cream together sugar and butter; add eggs and blend. In another bowl, sift spices with flour and alternately add flour mixture and buttermilk to creamed mixture; stir well after each addition. Fold in jam, raisins, pecans and walnuts. Pour batter evenly into three greased and floured 8-inch cake pans. Bake at 325° for 20 minutes or until toothpick inserted in the center comes out clean. Allow cake layers to cool in pans for 10 minutes; remove and place on wire rack to cool completely. Spread *Caramel Icing* on cake.

Caramel Icing

4 cups SUGAR, divided
1/2 lb. BUTTER

1 1/2 cups EVAPORATED
    MILK

In a saucepan, combine 3 1/2 cups of sugar with butter and milk and heat over low heat. In a small skillet, brown (caramelize) remaining 1/2 cup sugar and then add it to the saucepan mixture. Heat mixture to 232°, then beat until frosting consistency.

Guiness World Record Museum

This unique museum in Gatlinburg is the largest of the Guiness Museums in the U.S. It has 13 galleries and many exhibits detailing record-breaking phenomena that can be found in the Guiness Book of World Records.

Tennessee Gingerbread People

Todd O'Neal—Consumers Insurance, *Cooking with our Family* cookbook, La Vergne

1 cup packed BROWN SUGAR
1/3 cup SHORTENING
1 1/2 cups DARK MOLASSES
2/3 cup COLD WATER
7 cups ALL-PURPOSE FLOUR
2 tsp. BAKING SODA

2 tsp. GINGER
1 tsp. SALT
1 tsp. ALLSPICE
1 tsp. CLOVES
1 tsp. CINNAMON

In a bowl, combine brown sugar, shortening, molasses and water. Stir in remaining ingredients. Cover and refrigerate at least 2 hours. Heat oven to 350°. Roll dough out to 1/4-inch thickness on a lightly floured board. Cut with floured gingerbread man cutter. Place cookies 2 inches apart on a lightly greased cookie sheet and bake for 10-12 minutes or until no indentation remains when touched. Cool. Decorate as desired.

The "Overmountain Men"

Tennessee settlers played a vital part in winning the American Revolutionary War. The "Overmountain Men" helped to defeat the British at the Battle of King's Mountain (in the Carolinas), a victory which proved to be a major turning point in the war.

Pinto Bean Pie

"This recipe was created by a sharecropper's wife to use leftover beans. It tastes almost like a pecan pie. Very, very delicious!"

Shirley Woods—Cleveland

1/2 cup cooked, mashed
    PINTO BEANS
1 1/2 cups SUGAR
1 EGG
1 tsp. VANILLA

1 cup COCONUT
1 stick BUTTER or
    MARGARINE, melted
1 (9-inch) unbaked
    PIE SHELL

Preheat oven to 350°. In a bowl, combine all ingredients and mix well; pour into pie shell and bake for 45 minutes or until set.

Mamma's Caramel Pie

*"Whenever Mamma asked us what we wanted for Sunday
dessert, this was always our first choice!"*

Blanche Paty Catron—Lebanon

1 1/2 cups SUGAR	1 Tbsp. BUTTER
3 Tbsp. FLOUR	1 tsp. VANILLA
Dash of SALT	1 (9-inch) baked
3 EGG YOLKS	PIE SHELL
1 3/4 cups MILK	

In a bowl, mix together 1 cup sugar, flour and salt. In
another bowl, beat egg yolks, add milk and mix well. Combine
mixtures and blend. Add mixture to top of a double boiler and
cook until thickened to consistency of custard. In a heavy iron
skillet, brown 1/2 cup sugar to caramelized stage. Slowly stir
caramelized sugar into custard, stirring constantly until mixture is well blended and of desired thickness. Blend in butter
and vanilla. Pour custard into pie crust and spread ***Meringue***
to edges of top to seal. Bake pie at 325° for 10 minutes, or until
lightly browned.

Meringue

3 EGG WHITES	3 Tbsp. SUGAR
1/2 tsp. CREAM OF TARTAR	1/2 tsp. VANILLA

Combine egg whites and cream of tartar in a small bowl and
beat with electric mixer until peaks form. Slowly add sugar and
vanilla and continue to beat.

Murfreesboro

*The capital of Tennessee from 1819-1826,
this city lost the seat of government to Nashville by one vote!
Many interesting sites abound in the area including: Stones
River National Battlefield, Cannonsburgh Village, Sam
Davis Home, Fortress Rosecrans, Oaklands Historic House
Museum and Children's Discovery House Museum.*

Granny's Ice Cream

"This recipe won 2nd place in the Fayette County Dairy Contest."

Faye Hilliard—Glenn's Deer Processing, Somerville

3 EGGS, separated
1 cup SUGAR
1/4 tsp. SALT
1 tsp. VANILLA
1 can (14 oz.) SWEETENED
   CONDENSED MILK

1 can (12 oz.) EVAPORATED
   MILK
1/2 pt. WHIPPING CREAM,
   whipped
1/2 gal. SWEET MILK

In a bowl, beat egg yolks; add remaining ingredients except sweet milk and blend well. Stir in 1/2 of the sweet milk. Beat egg whites and fold into mixture. Add enough sweet milk to fill a 1-gallon electric or hand-crank freezer container. Freeze according to freezer directions.

Kingsport

Surrounded by mountains and incorporated in 1822, early Kingsport was known as "Boat Yard" because of its many wagon and flatboat freighting agencies. Visit historic Boat Yard Park which includes riverfront paths, a swinging bridge and the historic Netherland Inn.

Boiled Cookies

"These are a very popular Tennessee treat! You may use either smooth or crunchy peanut butter in this recipe."

Darlene Wilson—Newport

2 cups SUGAR
1 stick MARGARINE
1/2 cup MILK
4 Tbsp. COCOA

2 1/2 cups QUICK OATS
1/2 cup PEANUT BUTTER
2 tsp. VANILLA
1/2 cup chopped NUTS

In a saucepan, combine sugar, margarine, milk and cocoa. Bring to a boil and boil until hard balls form when dripped into cold water (about 1 1/2 minutes). Remove pan from heat and add remaining ingredients. Beat until well-blended and then drop by teaspoon onto wax paper. Let cool.

My Mother's Prune Cake

"This is an easy and quick cake to make. For variety, I some-times substitute blackberry or strawberry jam for the prunes."

Marjorie H. Hoffman—Lebanon

2 cups WHITE LILY®
  SELF-RISING FLOUR
1 1/2 cups SUGAR
1 1/4 tsp. BAKING SODA
1 tsp. NUTMEG
1 tsp. ALLSPICE
1 tsp. CINNAMON

3/4 cup VEGETABLE OIL
3 EGGS, beaten
1 cup BUTTERMILK
1 tsp. VANILLA
1 cup cooked PRUNES, finely
  diced or mashed
1 cup chopped PECANS

Grease and flour a 13 x 9 cake pan. Preheat oven to 325°. Sift together dry ingredients, then stir together all ingredients in order given. Pour batter into pan and bake 25-30 minutes. While cake is still hot and in pan, top with ***Buttermilk Glaze***.

Buttermilk Glaze

1 cup SUGAR
1 Tbsp. VANILLA
1/2 cup BUTTERMILK

1 Tbsp. WHITE CORN SYRUP
1 stick BUTTER or
  MARGARINE

Combine all ingredients in small saucepan; mix well and bring to a boil. Remove from heat.

Nashville's Stargazer

Edward Barnard of Nashville, a pioneer in celestial pho-tography, discovered 16 comets and Jupiter's 5th moon.

Granny's Skillet Cake

Kathy Stacy—Fall Branch

1/2 stick BUTTER
1/2 cup SUGAR
1 cup FLOUR

1/2 tsp. VANILLA
1 EGG
1/2 cup MILK

In a small iron skillet, melt butter, then pour it into a small mixing bowl. Stir in remaining ingredients and mix well. Pour back into same skillet. Bake at 400° for 20-25 minutes. Serve warm or cold.

Tennessee Stack Cake

"This recipe was passed down to me from my mother. It is definitely a family favorite."

Druceil K. Henry—Crossville

1 cup SUGAR
1 cup BUTTER
1 cup MOLASSES
2 EGGS
6 cups ALL-PURPOSE FLOUR

1 tsp. SALT
1/2 tsp. GINGER
1 tsp. BAKING SODA
1 Tbsp. BAKING POWDER
1/2 cup BUTTERMILK

In a bowl, cream together sugar and butter; beat in molasses and add eggs one at a time, beating well after each addition. In another bowl, combine flour, salt, ginger, baking soda and baking powder. Add flour mixture to creamed mixture alternately with buttermilk; blend thoroughly. Shape dough into 7 balls. On a well-floured surface, roll each ball out to a 9-inch circle. Place circles in greased 9-inch cake pans. Bake at 450° for 10 minutes. Allow layers to cool, then spread ***Apple Filling*** on top of each as you stack them. For best flavor, let cake stand for 24 hours before cutting.

Apple Filling

1 lb. dried APPLES
1/2 cup SUGAR
1 cup packed BROWN SUGAR

2 tsp. CINNAMON
1/2 tsp. CLOVES

In a saucepan, cover apples with water and cook over medium heat until soft. Remove apples to a bowl, mash and then blend in sugars and spices.

Oak Ridge

Oak Ridge was built during WWII for employees of the Clinton Engineering Works who worked on the Manhattan Project, which developed the first atomic bomb and nuclear reactor. CEW's successor, Oak Ridge National Laboratory, is one of the nation's largest federal multipurpose research and development centers.

Mamma's
Sweet Potato Pudding
"This was a favorite after school treat!"

Mary F. Cunnyngham—Cleveland

2 cups grated raw SWEET
  POTATOES
1 cup SUGAR
1 cup HALF AND HALF or MILK

2 EGGS, well beaten
1 Tbsp. BUTTER, melted
1 tsp. NUTMEG

In a bowl, combine sweet potatoes, sugar, half and half, eggs, butter and nutmeg and mix well. Pour into a well-greased pie pan. Bake at 350° for 30 minutes. Cut pudding into pie "wedges" and serve warm with *Orange Sauce*.

Orange Sauce

1 cup ORANGE JUICE   1/2 cup SUGAR   2 Tbsp. CORNSTARCH

In a saucepan combine orange juice, sugar and cornstarch and cook over low heat until thick and clear.

Apple Cobbler
"We have apple trees on our farm, so this is a popular recipe!"

Eunice Marie Smith—Pikeville

1/2 cup BUTTER or MARGARINE
1 1/2 to 2 cups SUGAR
2 cups WATER
1 1/2 cups sifted SELF-RISING
  FLOUR

1/2 cup SHORTENING
1/3 cup MILK
2 cups finely chopped
  APPLES
1 tsp. CINNAMON

Preheat oven to 350°. Melt butter in a 13 x 9 baking dish. In a saucepan, heat sugar and water until sugar melts. In a bowl, cut shortening into flour until crumbly. Add milk and stir with a fork only until dough leaves sides of bowl. Knead just until smooth. Roll dough out on a floured board to a 1/4" thick rectangle. Layer apples over top of dough and sprinkle with cinnamon. Roll dough up jelly roll style and seal edge with a little water. Cut dough into 16 slices; place in baking pan and pour sugar syrup over all. Bake 55-60 minutes or until golden brown.

Strawberry Nut Cake

"My mother used to pick her own strawberries to use in this cake. Although I now use frozen berries, this is still a very special cake in our family."

Phyllis K. Seay—Del Rio

1 box (18.25 oz.) WHITE CAKE MIX
1 box (6 oz.) STRAWBERRY JELL-O®
1 cup VEGETABLE OIL
1 cup frozen STRAWBERRIES
1/2 cup MILK
4 EGGS
1 cup COCONUT FLAKES
1 cup chopped NUTS

In a large mixing bowl, combine first 6 ingredients and beat with electric mixer for 2 minutes. Stir in coconut and nuts. Pour into three 8-inch greased and floured baking pans. Bake at 350° for 25-30 minutes. When cake is cool, spread ***Cream Cheese Icing*** between each layer.

Cream Cheese Icing

1 pkg. (8 oz.) CREAM CHEESE, softened
1 box (16 oz.) POWDERED SUGAR
1/2 can (12 oz.) EVAPORATED MILK

Mix cream cheese, powdered sugar and milk together in a small bowl and blend well.

Jackson

Settled in the early 19th century, Jackson became a railroading center—principally for cotton—by the 1850s and was a critical supply depot during the Civil War. Be sure to visit Casey Jones Village! Nearby Cypress Grove Nature Park has a 5,000-foot boardwalk that winds through 165 acres of cypress forest. The park is home to many native birds and animals as well as a birds-of-prey center.

Persimmon Pudding

"My grandmother and mother both made this pudding. This year I froze 10 pint boxes of the persimmon base so that I can make this tasty treat whenever I choose."

Louise B. Howard—Bulls Gap

1 pint PERSIMMON PUDDING BASE, defrosted
5 Tbsp. melted MARGARINE
1 EGG
1 1/2 cups packed BROWN SUGAR
1 1/2 cups SELF-RISING FLOUR

In a bowl, combine all ingredients thoroughly. Pour batter into a greased sheet cake pan; bake at 275° for 15-20 minutes.

Persimmon Pudding Base

1 gal. ripe PERSIMMONS   1 can (12 oz.) EVAPORATED MILK

Remove tops and tiny ends from persimmons and wash thoroughly. Place persimmons and evaporated milk in a large bowl and mash well. Run pulp through a colander to remove seeds and then place in pint-size freezer boxes and freeze.

Yields 5 pints.

Apple Fritters

Denise M. Ashworth—Hilltop House Bed & Breakfast Inn,
Greeneville

Batter:
1/2 cup ALL-PURPOSE FLOUR   1 EGG
Pinch of SALT   1/2 cup MILK
1 Tbsp. CANOLA OIL

3 GOLDEN DELICIOUS APPLES   OIL for cooking
FLOUR for dredging   POWDERED SUGAR

In a bowl, combine batter ingredients. Beat mixture until frothy, thick and smooth. Peel, core and slice apples 1/2-inch thick. Dredge apples in plain flour and then in batter. Heat cooking oil in skillet and cook apples until golden brown on both sides. Drain on paper towels. To serve, heat in microwave for 3 minutes then sprinkle with powdered sugar.

Apple Stack Cake

"My grandmother baked this cake, and now my mother and I bake it for my family. We always had orchards, so we picked our own apples and dried them to use in this cake."

Phyllis K. Seay—Del Rio

1/2 cup BUTTERMILK	2 EGGS
1 tsp. BAKING SODA	2 tsp. VANILLA
1 tsp. BAKING POWDER	5 cups FLOUR
1 cup SHORTENING	1 tsp. SALT
2 1/2 cups SUGAR	

In a small bowl, combine buttermilk, baking soda and baking powder and stir lightly. In a large bowl, cream together shortening and sugar; add eggs and vanilla and beat well. Stir in buttermilk mixture and blend. Sift flour and salt into creamed mixture and mix thoroughly; add enough flour to make dough easy to handle. Divide dough into 6-7 pieces; pat each piece into greased and floured 9-inch round cake pans. Bake at 425° for 10 minutes. Spread each cake layer with hot ***Apple Filling*** and stack layers on top of each other. Let cake stand at least 24 hours before slicing.

Apple Filling

1 lb. dried APPLES	1 tsp. CINNAMON
1/4 tsp. SALT	1 tsp. NUTMEG
2 cups SUGAR	1 tsp. CLOVES

In a saucepan, cover apples with water and cook over medium heat until apples are tender. Drain; mash apples and combine with remaining ingredients.

Jamestown's Notables

John Clemens, father of Samuel Clemens (Mark Twain), settled his family in this rural area in 1827. Another famous native, Sgt. Alvin C. York, World War I hero, was awarded the Congressional Medal of Honor. His family's home, the Alvin C. York Homeplace is a state historic area and open for tours.

Oakland Butterscotch Pie

"This dessert was served by the Oakland Community Club to soldiers coming home from World War I."

Cathrine Brown—Lebanon

5 cups packed BROWN SUGAR
1 cup FLOUR
1 1/2 cups BOILING WATER
4 EGGS
1 stick BUTTER
2 tsp. VANILLA

Pinch of SALT
12 baked individual
   PASTRY SHELLS
1 pt. WHIPPING CREAM
1/2 cup SUGAR

In a bowl, combine brown sugar and flour. Put mixture into iron skillet over medium heat; add water and blend well. In a separate bowl, slightly beat eggs and slowly add to sugar mixture, stirring constantly; add butter, vanilla and salt. Cook for 15-20 minutes until thickened. When cool, pour into pastry shells. Whip cream and sugar together and add a dollop to the top of each pie.

Great-Grandmother's Antique Chocolate Cake

"This cake recipe was handed down to us from Great-Grandmother Headington."

Vikki Woods—Iron Mountain Inn B & B and Creekside Chalet, Butler

2/3 cup SHORTENING
2 EGGS
1 cup WHITE SUGAR
1 cup packed BROWN SUGAR
2 2/3 cups FLOUR

1/4 tsp. SALT
2 tsp. BAKING SODA
4 Tbsp. COCOA
2 cups SOUR MILK*
2 tsp. VANILLA

In a bowl, cream together shortening, eggs and both sugars. Sift flour, salt, baking soda and cocoa together. Add dry ingredients to creamed mixture alternately with sour milk and vanilla. Bake in three 9-inch round or square pans for 25-30 minutes at 350°. When cool, frost as desired.

*To make sour milk, add 1 tablespoon vinegar to each cup of milk and set in warm water to sour.

Old-Fashioned Pound Cake

"My grandparents, Bertie and Alonzo Buttram, were home-steaders in Cumberland County. Grandpa could hardly wait for this cake to come out of the oven so he could have some while it was hot! He used to spread butter on his slice, even though the cake has a pound of butter in it!"

Ella D. Loveday—Crossville

1 lb. (2 cups) UNSALTED BUTTER, room temperature
1 lb. (2 cups) SUGAR
1 lb. (4 cups) SELF-RISING FLOUR
1 lb. (10 lg.) EGGS, room temperature
1 tsp. VANILLA

Preheat oven to 325°. In a mixing bowl, cream together butter and sugar with electric mixer for 8-10 minutes until very light and fluffy; add eggs, one at a time, beating for 1 minute after each addition. Gradually add 1 3/4 cups of the flour, pushing batter into beaters and scraping sides; beat for 1 minute. Gradually add remaining flour and vanilla, continuing to push batter into beaters and scraping sides; beat for 1 minute. Pour into 12-inch greased and floured tube pan. Bake cake for 1 hour and 5 minutes. Remove from pan immediately.

Chess Pie

"This recipe is over 100 years old. It was handed down to my husband's mother, Lillian Goddard Rawlings."

Gladys Fox Rawlings—Oak Ridge

1 Tbsp. FLOUR
1 cup SUGAR
1/2 cup BUTTER, melted
2 EGGS, slightly beaten

2 Tbsp. CREAM or MILK
1 tsp. VANILLA
Pinch of SALT
1 (9-inch) unbaked PIE SHELL

In a bowl, combine flour and sugar; add remaining ingredients and mix well. Pour mixture into pie shell. Bake at 325° for 30-45 minutes.

Peach Cheesecake Pie

"We have both peach and apple orchards and sell fresh fruit and pies at our store."

Marynell Breeden—Breeden's Orchard & Country Store, Mt. Juliet

1 can (14 oz.) SWEETENED
   CONDENSED MILK
1 pkg. (8 oz.) CREAM CHEESE
1/3 cup fresh LEMON JUICE

1 tsp. VANILLA
1 (9-inch) baked, deep-dish
   PIE CRUST
4 PEACHES, sliced

In a bowl, mix together condensed milk, cream cheese, lemon juice and vanilla. Pour mixture into pie crust; arrange peach slices on top. Pour **Peach Glaze** over all; refrigerate until serving time.

Peach Glaze

1/2 cup SUGAR
1/2 cup WATER

1 Tbsp. CORNSTARCH
1 PEACH, mashed

Combine all ingredients in a saucepan and cook, over medium heat, until thick and clear. Cool.

Peach Cobbler

Becky Arnott—Kingsport

3 cups sliced PEACHES
1 cup APPLESAUCE
1/2 tsp. CINNAMON
1 1/2 cups SUGAR
Juice of 1/2 LEMON
1 Tbsp. BUTTER
Dough for PIE CRUST

In a bowl, combine peaches, applesauce, cinnamon, sugar and lemon juice; layer in the bottom of a 10 x 8 glass baking dish. Dot butter over the top. Roll pie crust dough out to size of baking dish and arrange over top of peach mixture. Brush the top of the crust with a small amount of **CREAM** and sprinkle with **SUGAR**. Bake for 30 minutes at 425°.

The South's Best Coconut Cake!

"I like to prepare my own coconut for this cake rather than using the packaged versions."

Karan Bailey—Huckleberry Inn Bed & Breakfast, Sevierville

1 cup BUTTER, softened	1/4 tsp. SALT
2 cups SUGAR	1 cup MILK
4 EGGS	1 tsp. VANILLA
3 cups sifted CAKE FLOUR	1 tsp. ALMOND EXTRACT
1 Tbsp. BAKING POWDER	2 cups grated COCONUT*

Cream butter; gradually add sugar, beating well at medium speed with an electric mixer. Add eggs, one at a time, beating well after each addition. In another bowl, combine flour, baking powder and salt; add to creamed mixture alternately with milk, beginning and ending with flour mixture. Mix after each addition. Stir in vanilla and almond flavorings. Pour batter into 3 greased and floured 9-inch round cake pans. Bake at 350° for 25-30 minutes or until centers test done. Cool in pans for 10 minutes; remove from pans and cool completely. Place one layer on cake platter and spread with half of the ***Pineapple Filling,*** sprinkle 1/3 cup coconut over filling. Repeat with next layer. Spread ***Seven-Minute Frosting*** on top and sides of cake and sprinkle with remaining coconut.

Pineapple Filling

1 cup SUGAR	2 EGGS, beaten
3 Tbsp. ALL-PURPOSE FLOUR	2 Tbsp. LEMON JUICE
1 can (8 oz.) CRUSHED	1 Tbsp. BUTTER
PINEAPPLE, undrained	1 tsp. VANILLA

In a saucepan, combine sugar and flour; add remaining ingredients. Cook over medium heat, stirring constantly until thickened, about 2 minutes. Cool.

*See page 85.

(Continued on next page)

The South's Best Coconut Cake!
(Continued from previous page)

Seven-Minute Frosting

1 1/2 cups SUGAR
1/4 cup + 1 Tbsp. COLD
   WATER
2 EGG WHITES

1 Tbsp. LIGHT CORN
   SYRUP
Dash of SALT
1 tsp. VANILLA

Combine all ingredients except vanilla in top of a large double boiler. Beat at low speed with an electric mixer for 30 seconds or just until blended. Place over boiling water; beat constantly on high speed for 7 minutes or until stiff peaks form. Remove from heat. Add vanilla; beat 2 minutes or until thick enough to spread.

Preparing Coconut: Carefully pierce "eyes" of coconut with screwdriver or ice pick; drain liquid. Place coconut in a pan and heat in a 350° oven for 20-30 minutes or until cracks appear. Remove from oven; cool. Tap with hammer to open. Remove meat from shell and pare off dark skin with a vegetable peeler. Grate meat for cake.

Parson's Cake

"Years ago, there were 'visitation programs' during which the pastor and other men from the church would visit the homes of other parishoners. My husband raved about this cake from one of those visits. I got the recipe so I could make it for him."

Darlene Wilson—Newport

1 stick MARGARINE
1 cup SUGAR
2 EGGS
1/2 cup MILK
1/2 cup ORANGE JUICE

2 1/2 cups SELF-RISING
   FLOUR
1 Tbsp. VANILLA
1/2 cup chopped and floured
   CANDY ORANGE SLICES

Preheat oven to 350°. Grease and flour a tube pan. Cream margarine and sugar together; add eggs, beating well. Add milk, orange juice, flour and vanilla; beat well. Stir in candy. Pour batter into tube pan and bake for 50-60 minutes or until tests done. In a saucepan, bring **1 cup SUGAR** and **1/2 cup ORANGE JUICE** to a boil. Pour half of glaze over cake while still warm and in pan. Let set about 10 minutes, turn cake out onto serving plate and pour remaining glaze over top.

Apple Nut Cake

"This cake is a family favorite! It tastes best served the day after baking."

Sylvia M. Gregg—Newport

1 1/4 cups OIL
2 cups SUGAR
3 EGGS
3 cups FLOUR
1 tsp. SALT
1 tsp. BAKING SODA
1 tsp. CINNAMON
1 tsp. NUTMEG

1/2 tsp. CLOVES
3 cups peeled and
    chopped APPLES
1 cup RAISINS
1 cup COCONUT
1/2 cup NUTS
1 tsp. VANILLA

In a bowl, combine oil, sugar and eggs. Combine dry ingredients and mix with sugar and eggs. Using a wooden spoon, mix in remaining ingredients; pour into a well-greased and lightly floured Bundt pan. Bake for 1 hour at 350° or until tests done. While cake is still warm, drip ***Brown Sugar Glaze*** over top.

Brown Sugar Glaze

1/2 stick MARGARINE
1/2 cup packed BROWN SUGAR

3 Tbsp. MILK

Combine glaze ingredients in a saucepan, bring to a boil and boil for two minutes, stirring often.

Southern Pralines

Todd O'Neal—Consumers Insurance, *Cooking with our Family* cook book, La Vergne

2 sticks BUTTER
1/2 cup SUGAR
PECAN HALVES

1 box (16 oz.) GRAHAM
    CRACKERS

Place butter and sugar in a saucepan, bring to a boil and boil for 2 minutes. Place graham cracker squares on a cookie sheet; place one pecan half on top of each cracker. Spoon butter mixture over all. Bake 10 minutes in a 350° oven. Remove from sheet immediately and let cool.

Tennessee Bourbon Walnut Pie

Chef Karen Valentine—Christopher Place-An Intimate Resort, Newport

2 cups ALL-PURPOSE FLOUR
1 tsp. SUGAR
1/4 tsp. SALT
3/4 cup chilled UNSALTED BUTTER,
    cut into 1/2-inch pieces
1 lg. EGG
1 Tbsp. MILK

Blend flour, sugar and salt in food processor. Add butter and process using pulse method until mixture resembles coarse meal. In another bowl, whisk egg and butter to blend, add to processor and blend until moist clumps form. Gather dough into a ball and then flatten into a disk. Wrap in plastic and refrigerate for 1 hour. When ready to bake pie, preheat oven to 350°. Roll out dough on a floured surface to a 14-inch round; transfer to a 9-inch pie dish, fold edge under inside pie pan and crimp. Add *Tennessee Bourbon Walnut Filling;* bake about 55 minutes or until crust is golden and center of filling is set.

Tennessee Bourbon Walnut Filling

1 cup DARK CORN SYRUP
1/2 cup SUGAR
1 1/2 Tbsp. ALL-PURPOSE FLOUR
2 Tbsp. UNSALTED BUTTER, melted
2 Tbsp. TENNESSEE BOURBON

3 lg. EGGS
1 tsp. VANILLA
1/4 tsp. SALT
3/4 cup chopped WALNUTS
3/4 cup halved WALNUTS

In a bowl, whisk together all ingredients except walnuts. Mix in walnuts.

Henning
Visit the Alex Haley State Historic Site and Museum in this picturesque town of Victorian homes. Haley's childhood memorabilia and references to the people who inspired his characters in Roots *may be seen here.*

Mincemeat Cookies

"My aunt gave me this recipe. It's a family favorite."

Jacquie L. Dishner—Blountville

3/4 cup SHORTENING
1 1/2 cups SUGAR
3 EGGS, beaten
3 cups FLOUR
1 tsp. BAKING SODA
3/4 tsp. SALT
3 Tbsp. WATER

1 pkg. (9 oz.) DRY MINCEMEAT, finely crumbled
1 cup chopped NUTS
1 cup OATMEAL RAISIN CRISP® CEREAL
1 tsp. VANILLA

In a bowl, cream shortening; add sugar and eggs and beat until light and fluffy. In another bowl, sift flour, baking soda and salt together. Add 1/2 of the flour mixture to creamed mixture. Combine water and mincemeat, add to creamed mixture and blend well. Add nuts, cereal, remaining flour mixture and vanilla and combine all thoroughly. Drop by rounded teaspoons onto greased cookie sheet. Bake at 350° for 10 minutes. After baking, leave cookies on baking sheet for 5 minutes, then remove to rack to cool.

Tennessee Waltz

Written by Red Steward
Composed by Pee Wee King

I was waltzing with my darlin' to the Tennessee Waltz
When an old friend I happened to see
I introduced him to my loved one
and while they were waltzing
My friend stole my sweetheart from me.

I remember the night of the Tennessee Waltz
Now I know just how much I have lost
Yes I lost my little darlin' the night they were playing
The beautiful Tennessee Waltz.

Index

Index (Continued)

Index (Continued)

Index (Continued)

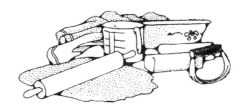

Tennessee Cook Book
Contributors

Becky Arnott, Kingsport 53, 63, 83
Debbie Bedingfield, Parsons 63
Dorothy H. Bowling, Knoxville 56
Breeden's Orchard & Country Store,
    Mt. Juliet 83
Cathrine Brown, Lebanon 14, 32, 81
Virginia Brown, Knoxville 13
Brenda Burke, Fall Branch 44
Mae Burke, Fall Branch 14, 32, 61
Calico Inn, Sevierville 21
Carriage Lane Inn, Murfreesboro 15
Casey Jones Home & Railroad Museum,
    Jackson 57
Blanche Paty Catron, Lebanon 73
Christopher Place-An Intimate Resort,
    Newport 40, 87
Consumers Insurance, La Vergne 72, 86
Ann Goode Cooper, Kingsport 66
Mary F. Cunnyngham, Cleveland 77
Nellie deBruycker, Crossville 26, 30
Mrs. Robert T. De Marcus, Knoxville 71
Jacquie L. Dishner, Blountville 88
Dollywood, Pigeon Falls 48
East Park Inn, An Urban Bed & Breakfast,
    Nashville 17, 58
East Tennessee State University, Johnson
    City 26, 51
Alison Ely, Lakeland 10, 29
Elvis Presley Enterprises, Inc., Memphis 42
Imogene M. Engle, Knoxville 27, 58, 69
Ernest Tubb Record Shop #1, Nashville
    28, 30
Debra Kay Evans, Erwin 62
Glenda Ezell, Lawrenceburg 61
Four Season's Market, Lebanon 54
Glenn's Deer Processing, Somerville 74
Sylvia M. Gregg, Newport 86
Druceil K. Henry, Crossville 51, 59, 76
Hillsboro House B & B, Nashville 16, 19
Hilltop House B & B Inn, Greeneville 79
Historic Rugby Visitor Ctr., Rugby 37, 66
Marjorie H. Hoffman, Lebanon 47, 75
Louise B. Howard, Bulls Gap 9, 79
Tena Huckleby, Greeneville 60

Huckleberry Inn B & B, Sevierville 24, 31,
    34, 84
Iron Mountain Inn B & B and Creekside
    Chalet, Butler 20, 81
Alease Irvine, Memphis 36
Jack Daniel's Dist., Lynchburg 9, 12, 13, 54
Jackson Ridge Orchard & Apple Cottage,
    Dandridge 65
Mrs. Waylon Jennings, Brentwood 25,
    33, 68
Brenda Kellow, Lebanon 43, 53
Ella D. Loveday, Crossville 52, 62, 82
Monteagle Inn, Monteagle 8, 22
Linda Moulton, Springfield 39, 50
National Chicken Council 41
National Cornbread Fest., S. Pittsburg 35
Carmela Peterson, Erwin 20, 70
Prospect Hill B & B Inn, Mountain City 18, 55, 64
Gladys Fox Rawlings, Oak Ridge 82
Judy Reaves, Greeneville 40
Phyllis K. Seay, Del Rio 78, 80
Shultz Farm Foods, Athens 11, 56
Eunice Marie Smith, Pikeville 77
Sharon Spears, Fall Branch 14, 19, 22
Kathy Stacy, Fall Branch 48, 75
Tina Stacy, Fall Branch 31
Dolores Y. Stevens, Knoxville 67
Tenn. Aquarium & IMAX 3D Theater,
    Chattanooga 8, 36
Tenn. Dept. of Ag., Nashville 46, 49
Tenn. Dept. of Tourist Dev., Nashville 37, 52
Tenn. Egg & Poultry Assn., Murfreesboro 23
Tennessee Hellspice, Newport 45
Tenn. Pork Producers Assn., Murfreesboro
    10, 11
Anita Urban, Moscow 50, 59
Shirley A. Viar, Dyersburg 49
Von Bryan Mountaintop Inn, Sevierville 24, 64
Virginia P. Waters, Lebanon 17
Linda Webb, Knoxville 7, 38
Annie Sue Whited, Lebanon 27, 38
Darlene Wilson, Newport 74, 85
Wilson Cnty Promotions, Inc., Lebanon 68
Shirley Woods, Cleveland 39, 72

More Cookbooks from Golden West Publishers

MISSOURI COOK BOOK

A tasty array of Show Me State favorites. Try *Vegetable Pancakes with Pesto Cream, Sweetbriar Baked Eggs & Mushrooms, Veggie-Ham Chowder, Beef Brisket Kansas City-Style,* and *Missouri Sugar Cured Ham.* Missouri facts and trivia too!

5 1/2 x 8 1/2 — 96 Pages . . . $6.95

KENTUCKY COOK BOOK

Recipes from all across the great state of Kentucky! Try *The Derby Café's Mint Julep,* a *Benedictine Sandwich* or *Kentucky Derby Pie!* Sample many other favorites too, like *Kentucky Hot Brown, Poke Sallet* or *Cabin Grits Fritters.* Includes Kentucky facts and trivia.

5 1/2 x 8 1/2 — 96 Pages . . . $6.95

FLORIDA COOK BOOK

Great recipes from the Sunshine State! Sample *Mango-Champagne Fritters* or *Baked Cheese Papaya, Ham-Tomato Quiche, Florida Blueberry Streusel Coffee Cake, Sautéed Gulf Coast Grouper, Crab & Cheese Pie* or *Drunken Shrimp.* Special Florida seafood section, tasty side dishes and delightful desserts. Includes fascinating facts and trivia.

5 1/2 x 8 1/2 — 96 pages . . . $6.95

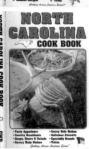

NORTH CAROLINA COOK BOOK

Filled with family favorites as well as recipes that showcase North Carolina's specialty foods. *Sausage Pinwheels, Shipwrecked Crab, Scuppernong Grape Butter, Carolina Blender Slaw, North Carolina Pork BBQ, Rock Fish Muddle, Hushpuppy Fritters, Hummingbird Cake, Peanut Butter Pie!*

5 1/2 x 8 1/2 — 96 pages . . . $6.95

VIRGINIA COOK BOOK

Over 140 recipes from all across this great state! From unbeatable seafood recipes to savory ham dishes, crab specialties, delicious apple recipes, tempting peanut delights and a cornucopia of historical and family favorites. Includes Virginia facts and trivia.

5 1/2 x 8 1/2 — 96 pages . . . $6.95

More Cookbooks from Golden West Publishers

BERRY LOVERS COOK BOOK

Over 120 delicious recipes featuring flavorful and nutritious berries! Try *Blueberry Buttermilk Muffins, Strawberry Peach Meringue Pie, Raspberry Dream Bars, Blackberry Summer Salad* or *Boysenberry Mint Frosty* and many more. Tempting recipes for all occasions. Includes berry facts and trivia!

5 1/2 x 8 1/2 — 96 pages . . . $6.95

APPLE LOVERS COOK BOOK

Celebrating America's favorite—the apple! 150 recipes for main and side dishes, appetizers, salads, breads, muffins, cakes, pies, desserts, beverages and preserves, all kitchen-tested by Shirley Munson and Jo Nelson.

5 1/2 x 8 1/2 — 120 Pages . . . $6.95

CORN LOVERS COOK BOOK

Over 100 delicious recipes! Try *Corn Chowder, Corn Soufflé, Apple Cornbread* or *Caramel Corn,* to name a few. You will find a tempting recipe for every occasion in this collection. Includes corn facts and trivia too!

5 1/2 x 8 1/2 — 88 pages . . . $6.95

EASY RECIPES for WILD GAME and FISH

By hunter-traveler-cook Ferne Holmes. More than 200 "wild" recipes for large and small game, wild fowl, fish and side dishes. By Ferne Holmes, author of *Easy RV Recipes.*

5 1/2 x 8 1/2 – 60 Pages . . . $6.95

BEST BARBECUE RECIPES

A collection of more than 200 taste-tempting recipes.
• Marinades • Rubs • Mops • Ribs • Wild Game
• Fish and Seafood • Pit barbecue and more!

5 1/2 x 8 1/2—144 pages . . . $6.95

ORDER BLANK

GOLDEN WEST PUBLISHERS

☼ 4113 N. Longview Ave. • Phoenix, AZ 85014

www.goldenwestpublishers.com • **1-800-658-5830** • FAX 602-279-6901

Qty	Title	Price	Amount
	Apple Lovers Cook Book	**6.95**	
	Berry Lovers Cook Book	**6.95**	
	Best Barbecue Recipes	**6.95**	
	Chili-Lovers' Cook Book	**6.95**	
	Chip and Dip Cook Book	**6.95**	
	Corn Lovers Cook Book	**6.95**	
	Easy Recipes for Wild Game & Fish	**6.95**	
	Joy of Muffins	**6.95**	
	Kentucky Cook Book	**6.95**	
	Missouri Cook Book	**6.95**	
	North Carolina Cook Book	**6.95**	
	Pecan Lovers Cook Book	**6.95**	
	Pumpkin Lovers Cook Book	**6.95**	
	Quick-Bread Cook Book	**6.95**	
	Secrets of Caveman Cooking	**6.95**	
	Tennessee Cook Book	**6.95**	
	Tequila Cook Book	**7.95**	
	Texas Cook Book	**6.95**	
	Veggie Lovers Cook Book	**6.95**	
	Virginia Cook Book	**6.95**	

Shipping & Handling Add: United States $4.00
Canada & Mexico $6.00—All others $13.00

☐ My Check or Money Order Enclosed

☐ MasterCard ☐ VISA

Total $ _____

(Payable in U.S. funds)

Acct. No. _____ Exp. Date _____

Signature _____

Name _____ Phone _____

Address _____

City/State/Zip _____

Call for a FREE catalog of all of our titles

11/03 **This order blank may be photocopied**

Tenn. Ck. Bk.